Counselling Older Clients

Counselling Older Clients

Ann Orbach

SAGE Publications
London • Thousand Oaks • New Delhi

First published 2003

 SAGE Publications Ltd
6 Bonhill Street
London EC2A 4PU

SAGE Publications Inc.
2455 Teller Road
Thousand Oaks, California 91320

SAGE Publications India Pvt Ltd
B-42, Panchsheel Enclave
Post Box 4109
New Delhi 100 017

British Library Cataloguing in Publication data

A catalogue record for this book is available from the British
Library

ISBN 0 7619 6405 3
ISBN 0 7619 6406 1 (pbk)

Library of Congress Control Number: 2003102952

Typeset by C&M Digitals (P) Ltd., Chennai, India
Printed and bound in Great Britain by Athenaeum Press, Gateshead

'Old age hath yet his honour and his toil'
Tennyson

Contents

Introduction

My interest in working with older people began quite by chance, when I was in my 50s and a colleague asked me if I would see an 'old lady' of 79. I never thought of refusing though I was full of doubts, having assumed that people of her age could not benefit from what I had to offer. Up till then my clients had all been middle-aged or young, many of them students. I see now that I had been imbued, quite unknowingly, with most of the ageist attitudes that I vehemently attack in this book. But there was also humility. How could I hope to help people of my parents' generation, whose experiences of the world and of themselves were so far ahead of mine?

During our first session, my client and I were both equally nervous. She sat on the edge of her chair and looked up at me expectantly. I felt as though I was with a shy schoolgirl, eager to learn. Very soon, as we began to feel at home with each other, we seemed to become ageless, and the sessions timeless. She was looking for a mother-figure, and we were neither of us surprised by this reversal of roles. We worked together for several years. There was no reason to limit the time, and, although I have since then taken on people for an agreed shorter period, I will always be grateful to that first older client for all she taught me, and all that both of us were able to explore about growing old.

It has been my involvement since 1996 in founding SAGE (Senior Age) Counselling Service in my locality that has heightened my interest and expanded my experience in working with this age group. The original idea was not mine but I found myself called on to implement it, and the opportunity arose when I was asked to run a workshop at a Diocesan Conference on Old Age and Death. A group of counsellors attended and this included at least two who had already done some work counselling older people. One of these, Chrystabelle Brotherton, has given me permission to publish the case history which you will find in Chapter 3 of this book. After the conference, a group of us started meeting to discuss the idea and, the following autumn, SAGE was launched. It took a long time getting off the ground, and longer still for people to believe in it as a viable project, but we have made ourselves known through various forms of publicity and twice-yearly study days, and last year we achieved charitable status. So the work goes ahead and we learn from each other, both in a counselling and supervisory capacity.

You will find, in reading what follows, that I use the words counselling and psychotherapy more or less interchangeably. When, more than ten years ago, I used to tutor students at Chichester Counselling Services, I would have seen a gap between the two. Counselling training in those days was squeezed into two years, and I had to fit the psychodynamic input into year two and also include seminars on transactional analysis (TA), gestalt and sex therapy, given by invited seminar leaders. These days, with the enormous growth of trainings, many of them up to degree standard, counselling is a profession in its own right. Although some of my former students have subsequently trained as psychotherapists, this is no longer seen as a necessary progression to superior status. In a publication on counselling and psychotherapy in primary health care, the authors state:

> The task of differentiating between counselling and psychotherapy is almost impossible, given the many different meanings that are attributed to both terms, as well as the overlap between them ... Struggling to make distinctions in meaning between terms takes us into stormy waters, where the rivalries and status positions among different training organisations can seriously interfere with clarity of thinking. (Wiener and Sher, 1993: xxiii)

The case histories I have included, though based on real people, with real people's problems, have, for the sake of confidentiality, been so radically altered as to make them fictitious. There are two exceptions, as shown clearly in the text, where counsellors have offered me exact scripts of their counsellor/client interactions.

It has been easier to find a group of counsellors to form a specialised service such as SAGE than I imagine it would have been to choose a group of psychotherapists. My impression is that counsellors tend to be more pragmatic in how they are prepared to work, and generally more eclectic in using the various models they have learnt, in order to suit particular client needs. Humanistic and psychodynamic counsellors work well together in discussing client problems, enriching each other and also the supervisor. I hope some of their easy eclecticism comes over in the text of this book. I hope also that what I have written may prove helpful to any counsellors and counselling students who are interested in exploring what it is like to be old and how we can creatively be of help to people who have lived much longer than ourselves.

My aim is to expand the counselling field by including the whole spectrum of human development from youth to old age and showing that it is never too late for growth and change. This is borne out by experience as I illustrate in the following chapters. I explore some of the assumptions that have, in the past, written off the over 60s as unsuitable clients, and the generalisations that continue to work against accepting them as still developing individuals with specific problems. I go on to discuss suitable counsellors and whether their ways of working will need adjustment to address an older person's needs. There is a chapter on relationships and on sex in later life. Another chapter discusses the problems of older people from ethnic minorities, those who are disabled and those who are gay. I look at the importance of older people's life stories and how we can help make sense of them. How people cope with loss will be found to overshadow each chapter, particularly loss through retirement, bereavement, disability and the approach of death. Suggestions for reflection and discussion are included at the end of each chapter.

The book may be of interest to anyone caring for older people, both professionally and in a family context, but it is particularly aimed at counsellors and student counsellors, who are interested in exploring what it is like to be old and how we can creatively be of help to people who have lived longer than ourselves.

My background is analytical psychotherapy. I qualified with the Guild of Psychotherapists in the 1970s, having studied Freud, Jung and object relations theory – all psychodynamic – with a smattering of existentialism thrown in. Probably this early bias still shows in my writing, even though, for many years, I have supervised therapists and counsellors from humanistic and integrative backgrounds.

I would like to dedicate this book to past and present members of SAGE Counselling Service.

1

Age Affirmative Practice

How can counsellors develop a positive approach to older clients in an age-unfriendly world? In this chapter, I shall attempt to answer that question.

We need to challenge ageism in all its forms, not least that which has been internalised by the people whom we are hoping to affirm. We need to help our clients in distingishing between problems which have been projected on to them by younger people's expectations and those that are intrinsic to the stages of development they are passing through. Counselling is not about control but empowerment. A weakened body does not necessarily mean a weakened mind, and our treatment will only be affirmative if we are able to show respect for our clients as having survived a century of extraordinarily fast change, and as having gained enough wisdom to promote a balance of power between themselves and us. We need to be open and humble enough to learn from them as much as they can learn from us.

Living longer

Our population is ageing at an unprecedented pace. 'By the year 2030, if the gerontologist, Tom Kirkwood is right, there will be 35,000 people in this country over the age of 100' (Vaughan, 2002). The Government Actuary's Department (GAD) is cautious in its predictions but highlights the fact that the ratio of old to young is undergoing considerable change:

> ... in 1998 there were nearly 1.4 million (13 per cent) more children under 16 than people of pensionable age. However by 2008 the population of pensionable age is projected to exceed the number of children. (GAD, 1998)

Longer-term predictions suggest that the number of people over pensionable age will peak at 16 million by 2040. We are also moving later into middle age, which has traditionally been estimated as about 36 (with or without a mid-life crisis) but projected to rise to 41 by 2021 and reach a stable 44 in about 40 years time.

Individuals age at different rates and it would be senseless to lump all pensioners together and write them off as old. There are two generations spanning the time between retirement and death – 30 years from 60 to 90. The terms 'young old' and 'old old' are useful in describing two different stages of the ageing process, though I prefer not to designate a particular age at which people pass into old old-age. We often meet people who are old at 40 and others in their 80s and 90s with continuing youthful attitudes.

Discrimination

Although we live in a society where considerable attention is being paid to human rights and the removal of restrictive labels, it seems that we still inhabit a prejudiced environment.

Research by Age Concern uncovered evidence of age discrimination at all levels of the NHS. A Gallup poll in 1999 showed that 1 in 20 people over 65 had been refused treatment, while 1 in 10 had been treated differently after the age of 50. This included 40 per cent of coronary care units attaching age restrictions to the use of clot-bursting drug therapy, the refusal of kidney dialysis or transplants to 66 per cent of kidney patients aged 70–79 and no invitations to breast screening for women of 65 and over. There were also delays in hip replacements, the withdrawal of chiropody services and inappropriate use of anti-psychotic drugs in care homes. Despite government asurances of equal treatment, the evidence from patients and their relatives showed that discrimination was widespread and, in many cases, hospitals were failing to provide essential care. Although many patients in the survey spoke when invited to, others suffered in silence. 'Many people of my generation see doctors as gods and would never contradict them. Or they're frightened' (Gilchrist, 1999: 3). Old people come to feel that they are expendable. Treatments that are available to younger patients are withheld because of shorter life expectancy. Decisions are made on the basis of productivity. Whereas the young have something to contribute to society, the old are seen as a burden and a drain.

Things have had to go from bad to worse before a turning point could be hoped for. An 88 year-old, rushed to hospital after a stroke, was left on a trolley in a corridor for several hours, then moved to a mixed ward and eventually to a geriatric ward, where her relatives found her in much distress, lying in her own faeces. The stroke had taken away her voice, so she had no way of complaining except by writing notes which no one read. 'What she didn't know was that doctors had written "Do not resuscitate" on her file' (*The Observer*, 1/4/2001). This was not unusual, but the fate of many like her. When *The Observer* published details of her case, there was a response from hundreds of readers with stories of their elderly relatives receiving similar treatment. What followed was the 'Dignity of the Ward' campaign and a pledge by the Government to end ageism in hospitals. The NHS is now committed to providing care 'regardless of age and on the basis of clinical need alone'. This is a welcome step in the right direction but:

> Many specialists now believe ageism is so entrenched that it will take more than a blueprint, however radical, and a set of targets, however ambitious to transform the culture of a lack of respect for the elderly. (Ibid.)

The word 'ageism' is comparatively new (Butler, 1975) but the prejudice has earlier roots and seems to be a phenomenon of Western culture, with its emphasis on a person's usefulness and productivity. Here, in the West, we have all but lost sight of some of the spiritual values that still hold sway in less materialistic cultures. Those psychologists concerned with studying human development might benefit from the insights of Confucian philosophy in which each stage of life has meaning.

> At 40, I was free from doubt. At 50, I understood the laws of Heaven. At 60, my ear was docile. At 70, I could follow the desire of my heart without transgressing the right. (Soothill, 1910 quoted in Featherstone and Wernick, 1985: 149–50)

The following quote looks like a caricature, yet contains some uncomfortable grains of truth about how the young look at the old.

> He or she is white-haired, inactive, unemployed, making no demands on anyone, docile in putting up with loneliness, rip-offs of every kind and boredom, and able to live on a pittance. He or she … is slightly deficient in intellect and tiresome to talk to … asexual, because old people are incapable of sexual activity, and it is unseemly if they are not. He or she is unemployable because old age is second childhood and everyone knows that the old make a mess of simple work. Some credit points can be gained by meeting or being nice to these subhuman individuals, but most of them prefer their own company and the company of other aged unfortunates. Their main occupations are religion, grumbling, reminiscing and attending the funerals of friends. (Comfort, 1977: 2)

Ageism associates growing old with unstoppable physical decline, and views any evidence of vitality in older people as exceptional rather than the norm. Not only joints and muscles, but also mental capacities, are expected to fail. Old people's pain tends to be treated with palliative drugs instead of probing for causes, while those who suffer from depression are given anti-depressants and are unlikely to be referred for counselling.

Individuals working with old people may have consciously overcome their own prejudices but are likely to be affected by those of the organisations for which they work, where ageism may be endemic within the general ethos of the care-giving work-place, often without any of those concerned being aware that this is so. Ageism, as already mentioned, seems to pervade the NHS, not only in medical treatments but also in the way old people are nursed and spoken to. Being hard of hearing or in shock is too often interpreted as senility. 'You mean your mother isn't senile', said a young doctor to the daughter of a 90 year-old, who had been trying for some time to protect her mother from humiliation. 'You never bothered to find out', was the reply. In homes for old people, whether NHS or private, dependency is too often taken for granted, and efforts on the part of residents to hold on to their self-respect are seen as stubborn or 'naughty'. The carers tend to be brisk and lack the patience to watch people slowly doing tasks for themselves which could be more quickly got through by those in charge.

Paul Terry has written about his time as clinical psychologist and counsellor in a long-stay geriatric hospital. He worked with staff as well as patients and gained important insights into how institutions work, especially on an unconscious level. The nursing staff would protect themselves from the pain of continuous contact with old-age and death by various unconscious mechanisms of withdrawal, with the result that they built up defences instead of overcoming anxiety in constructive ways.

> Change, however much wanted, is likely to be resisted because it means giving up the familiar, experiencing the unknown and having to learn from experience. (Terry, 1997: 100)

He mentioned the institutional defences which get in the way of individual caring and also contribute to the institutionalising of the patients, which leads to passivity and decline.

It is hardly surprising that neglect and disrespect in old age often produce the knock-on effect of old people ceasing to believe in their worth as human beings. This internalised bias against themselves may find fertile ground in a person's inner world, already shaped by the rules of a strictly disciplined upbringing. Older women have not been encouraged to stand up for themselves and vaunt their abilities. Men have moulded their characters to accord with social expectations of manliness and never giving into weakness. When expectations fall away and society sees only failing strength, disempowerment is bound to follow. These people have no in-built mechanisms against discrimination. Their own ageing creeps up on them surreptitiously. They do not feel different, nor do they feel old, unless jerked into a sudden realisation that other people – perhaps even their younger friends and family – are perceiving them as in the old-age category. They have no pride in age and no defence against it (Scrutton, 1998). So they accept their ageing and internalise ageist attitudes, with depressing results.

Age-related problems – transitions

The advice that I find myself wanting to give counsellors with their older clients is the one given to me by a supervisor when I first took on a woman of 80 – treat her like anyone else. This is sound advice in that it warns us against the prejudiced attitude of regarding our elders as a different species. But, if we think about it, we will come to realise that the problems of childhood and adolescence, although they continue to affect the mature adult, are nevertheless not intrinsically the same as those of adulthood, but specific to the age group concerned, often relating to how a person copes with transitions. Getting old has much in common with reaching adolescence in that it involves moving to a further stage in our life span. Instead of growing up and embracing new experience, the older adult's continued growth may best be achieved by integrating the various strands of a life-time's knowledge, and working towards the wisdom that can be derived from the changes and trials that had to be passed through.

Part of a counsellor's affirmation will be helping the client to let go of ego-centred desires and become aware of valued parts of the self that can be passed on to future generations. None of this need be viewed in a negative light. There is still growth before death, and, even in a shrinking future, there is room for hope.

Transitions invariably result in loss, for instance:

Retirement: loss not only of the daily routine of work, but also the loss of earning power. Financial status is particularly a problem for those having to rely on the state pension.

Bereavement: the most obvious loss, not only of a person's partner but contemporary friends. Each bereavement is a reminder of everyone's mortality.

Loneliness: having to live alone, perhaps for the first time, without anyone on hand for sharing thoughts and memories.

Parental Role: Not only do children leave home, but there may eventually be role reversal, the children becoming the parents' carers and the parents feeling that they are a burden to their children.

Declining Health: loss of energy, mobility, and the depression that goes with it.

Failing Memory: the fear – and sometimes reality – of dementia.

Unresolved Conflicts: the realisation that old quarrels can no longer be mended, particularly in cases where one of the protagonists has died.

Facing the Reality of Death: having to let go of life itself – a final loss.

Adjusting to transitions, accepting loss, eventually letting go of the future – these will be the themes of this book. We probably all know resilient old people, who are able to overcome these problems; some seem to achieve serenity. But these are not the ones who are likely to become our clients.

In a climate of ageism, it is vitally important that counsellors accept their ageing clients as individuals, and help them to reject the 'isms' that reduce them to stereotypes.

Many ageing people are trapped into prescriptive patterns, and counselling should help them to understand better what old age is in their own experience rather than what elderly stereotypes tell us old age should be. (Scrutton, 1998: 34)

Empowerment

Counsellors need to watch the balance of power between them and their clients, individuals who are sometimes, though not always, physically frail, even a little slow, but they are not children and should not be treated as such. We need always to remember their seniority, in experience as well as in years, and to respect the authority that used to be theirs, both at work and in the home. These are people who were brought up to esteem their elders. Now, in our changed environment, their younger carers treat them in such a free and easy manner that perhaps they are missing the respect they hoped to have earned in their old age.

They may look up to their counsellors as experts, not knowing quite what to expect, but hoping that some of their problems can be solved.

This puts us in a position of power, which can either be used or abused. We need to look into ourselves and to do our best to root out any trace of prejudice that we may have absorbed from an ageist society. We should try to imagine ourselves in the clients' position – remembering that it will be ours one day – and adapt ourselves to their older way of being. I strongly advise against the use of first names unless, or until, the client gives permission. The first-name habit has permeated hospitals and other institutions during the last few decades and is supposed to show friendliness but, to an older age group, it may give a different message, that of being 'talked down to'. Addressing one of them as 'love' or 'dear' is equally unacceptable.

Carl Rogers, in developing client-centred therapy, introduced the idea of therapists as 'quiet revolutionaries' (Rogers, 1978), providing opportunities for clients' 'self-ownership', and encouraging individuals to rely on their personal power in making decisions, rather than on outside authority. I see this 'quiet revolution' that we need to undertake as part of a continuing struggle against all the discrimination and stereotyping that I have been describing. In this way, counselling could be seen as working subversively against the established order. Nevertheless, in practice, most of us are not revolutionary. We accept that counselling needs structure if it is to be recognisably therapeutic and not chat or pep talk. The counsellor sets out the rules of when and where to meet, how often and for how long, as well as imposing boundaries, not of the client's making. This would seem to limit a client's self-ownership, but leaves him or her with the important decision of whether to come for counselling at all and the power to stop at any time. There is also the assurance of confidentiality, as one of the most important boundary issues. In acknowledging our limits, all we can do is explain how and why they have been developed as part of the setting and context in which we work, and that we will explore together just how much freedom of choice can, in fact, be enjoyed and how much power realistically belongs to the client.

And yet, we face a contradiction:

> There is always a delicate balance within counselling between the requirement that the counsellor is personally powerful, in the sense meant by Rogers (1978), and the danger of being oppressive, of putting unseen pressure on the client to conform to some set of norms and values. What is the point of going to see a counsellor unless they have the potential to have a powerful impact on your life? (McLeod, 1998: 260–1)

Loss and gain

Sometimes it looks as though old age is all about loss, and, with a severely depressed client, the counsellor may get caught in a downward spiral. The negative side of empathy is that we take on the old person's problems as our own and there seems no escape from increasing weakness, fatigue and pessimism. How, we wonder, can anything improve in this client's limited future. And, in the long run, will our own lives just peter out and become meaningless? Questions like these underline our own need for therapeutic help (either individually or in a group) in order to explore what, for us, radiates meaning. Through concentration on our life's goals and our hopes for people we care for, we may become aware that, though these goals may undergo changes as we get older, they need not vanish without trace. Those clients, who have been high achievers in the past, may perhaps be able to relax and bask in their success, or they may still be striving to realise impossible ambitions. Others may feel they have failed in what they wanted to do and blame both themselves and other people. What is important for us, who counsel them, is to help them bring the past into the present, with the acknowledgement that they can no longer hope to save the world, but may, within realistic limits, work towards lesser goals that are still worth pursuing. Despite pain and illness, there can be an inner strength, and a realisation that the nearness of death 'can enhance the perception of meaningfulness by making life more precious, precisely because of its limitation in time' (Tomer, 2000: 285).

Reflection and review

- I have emphasised in this first chapter how much prejudice surrounds ageing people in our society. Do you agree that ageist attitudes could undermine programmes of counselling for this age group?
- Think about instances of ageism that you have encountered – at work, in the media, in yourself. Can you be honest about your own prejudices?
- Think about the concept of 'internalised ageism'. One of our aims, as counsellors, could be to restore a person's 'self-ownership'. How do you understand this term?
- In what ways do you think you could affirm an ageing client who is anxious about counselling? How would you explain the process to him/her?
- Discuss with your colleagues how you see the balance of power between counsellor and client.
- The structure of the counselling situation inevitably reinforces the power of the counsellor. How could you make sure that this power is not abused?
- Think about what life means to you and perhaps discuss this with a friend or therapist. How do you think your own insight might help you in counselling a client who is old and depressed?

2

Counsellors, Clients and Settings

In this chapter, I describe counselling in old age as pioneer work, and I discuss what sort of counsellors should be considered suitable. Then I look at likely clients, their ages, background and history. I mention services that have been set up to specialise in this work, including one in Sussex with which I have been involved. I point out that counsellors often have to visit clients in their own homes, rest homes or hospitals, and the difficulties that may arise in these different settings. I give some examples to show how problems develop and the importance of supervision, both as support and further training.

Choosing counsellors

Working with older people is specialised work for which certain personal qualities are needed, though not necessarily a lot of extra training. There are many spheres in working with older people where being young is an advantage. Youthful looks and energy are welcomed, for instance, in occupational therapy, some of the art therapies, nursing and general caring. But counsellors are seen – always to some extent – as authority figures, knowledgable, wise, reliable and able to take on the full force of the clients' fear and pain, as well as the burden of their intimate secrets. This work is for mature counsellors, already qualified and in general counselling practice. I would choose those who, either at work or in their families, have had experience of being with ageing people. Some come from nursing or social work backgrounds or have been wardens in sheltered housing complexes. On average, the counsellors chosen are middle-aged, and they often have elderly parents with whose age-specific problems they are having to cope. They need to be flexible enough to be able – under careful supervision – to adapt some of the hard and fast rules learnt in their initial training, especially when visiting clients in hospitals or in their own homes. Common sense mixed with compassion is often worth more than a head full of psychological theory. I have always believed that theory should issue from practice rather than practice having to fit with textbook expectations, and was glad to find this thinking corroborated in the journal *Psychodynamic Counselling*, in an article that favours 'practice-led theory' as more important than 'ossified' printed words.

In this way the trainee will concentrate on her struggle to find a personal language in which to describe and examine her experience and engagement with the client. She will employ and develop a kind of personal critique in which her own imagery and metaphoric vocabulary will serve to enable her to get inside the meaning of therapeutic encounters. (Gross, 1999: 123)

Experience of life is as important as clinical experience. Sometimes the best-equipped counsellors are those who have had traumas of their own and have been able to integrate them in their personal therapy. They must be able imaginatively to look ahead to their own ageing and death. They should be emotionally mature and give evidence of psychic health, that is they can own and take responsibility for their thoughts and feelings, acknowledge any deep-seated prejudices and be able to work through them. The hope in any counselling service is that it will include both male and female counsellors. The reality is that most are female, white, middle-aged and middle-class. A cultural mix should be welcomed and facilitated whenever possible.

The above applies whether matching counsellor and client in general counselling practice, or in special services set up to cater for the old. The latter are pioneer projects, sometimes under the umbrella of Age Concern. It is unusual for such services to train their counsellors from scratch, but further training should be encouraged through supervision, reading and study days.

Clients — who are they?

Invariably, they are pensioners, but include a huge age range, between 60 and 90 plus. It is not really possible to name any particular age at which people become old.

What sort of world did these clients grow up in? Central to their experience was the second World War. Some were still children. They may have been evacuated to save them from being bombed in the big cities that bore the brunt of the blitz. This often meant leaving their parents and having to live with strangers and get used to different customs. Or they may have stayed at home with the constant threat of bombs, and, in some cases, being 'bombed out' of their houses. Others were in their teens when war broke out and found their adolescence disrupted; some felt that it was taken away from them and they had to be serious and grow up quickly. Higher education was often disrupted. There was conscription for both men and women. All sorts of emotions would have been experienced – excitement, fear, frustration, shock. Some broke free from conventional restraints. There was a big social mix-up. There was also the beginning of what later became the sexual revolution. What sort of legacy did that leave? What effects may still persist?

Some had terrifying experiences. There are still survivors of the holocaust, who may have been children at the time, and somehow managed to live through it. Others were starved and tortured in Japanese prison camps and were unable to talk about their experiences, sometimes for as long as 40 or 50 years. There were pilots involved in the saturation bombing of German cities, such as Dresden, who were haunted much later by what they had done.

These are some of the people needing counselling today and gradually becoming aware that the 'talking cure' works. To others, the war was the most exciting time of their lives and nothing so interesting has happened since. But the young don't want to hear – 'Dad's a war bore'. These old people want someone to listen to their stories.

Those who were children in the 1930s, lived through the war, the drab, and still rationed, post-war years, the swinging 60s, and into the computer age, have either adapted remarkably to accelerating change or felt themselves left behind, overtaken by technology. These may be our clients.

Perception of time changes. Those who are old, retired and slowing down, experience long pauses in which to ruminate, to mourn, to worry about their changing bodies, to be lonely and wish for company, and to be bored. Activities take longer; much less gets done. Although, on some days, time hangs heavily, on others it runs away. The inefficient body is accepted as old, but the inner thoughts and feelings are recognisably the same as they always were, and the past glows with more clarity than the present. Now life moves fast-forward – days, weeks, months, and birthdays following hard on each other's heels. Difficult to believe that one has suddenly become the oldest in the family.

Bodily changes can be as disconcerting as those of adolescence. Multiple bereavements bring various degrees of depression. Hopes diminish. Fears increase. Who can possibly help? No one seems to have the time. The old advice was 'pull yourself together', but what is the good of that when falling apart?

These are our clients – if they can be persuaded to seek help. Counselling is quite a new option. There was nothing like it in their younger days. Even now, they murmur, it is surely only for the young – mixed-up teenagers, drug addicts, those infected with HIV. Being old is just something you have to put up with.

How can we respond?

The answer has to be with more publicity, for the needs, and also the abilities, of potential clients to be understood, and for them to have their voices heard. The fight against ageism and discrimination in all spheres of public life needs to go on. The counselling service, geared towards senior age (SAGE), which I helped to found in Sussex, took a long time to get off the ground. We distributed leaflets, gave talks, advertised study days and spread the word around. Now, after six years, we are getting better known and clients are coming regularly, though in trickles, not in floods. The first few years were a struggle but the trickle of clients never quite dried up. There are similar agencies in other parts of the country. Recent media treatment of old age (newspapers and television) have given more positive messages than formerly. So perhaps there is reason for hope.

Settings

These tend to be more various than is usual, in that the counsellor often has to go to the client rather than the client to the counsellor. Clients may be counselled in their own homes, in hospitals or rest homes or, if they are sufficiently mobile, in pre-arranged rented quarters that the counsellor is able to use. Home or hospital visits are inclined to pose a threat to the boundaries normally observed in counselling practice, and we need to be extra careful in defining the difference between professional and social meetings. Punctuality is important, as is the consistency of the setting. Sometimes there is no choice of room, though the counsellor can make suggestions about where they are likely to be least disturbed and whether (if in the client's home), there is some way for the telephone to be left unanswered, and visits from friends discouraged during the counselling hour. The client, playing host, will probably offer cups of tea. These should, as a rule, be tactfully declined, with the explanation that serving and drinking tea would be a distraction from the purpose of the session. This may upset the client, who, in some cases, feels that tea and cake is the only payment she is able to offer. Bearing in mind that flexibility is important, it is always worth discussing in supervision whether, in particular cases, it is more therapeutic to break a rule than rigidly to keep it. One may be visiting someone who is losing sight or hearing, so it is advisable to sit where one can be seen and not in silhouette. Speaking slowly and distinctly is obviously important, and, of course, no shouting. If what one says seems not to be getting through, it should be re-worded. This advice seems obvious, but not every counsellor finds it easy to adapt her style – hence my advice about choosing counsellors who are used to being with elderly people. Textbook jargon should, of course, be taboo. One needs to adapt one's language to the client's and avoid too many purely modern idioms. As regards seating arrangements, it is important for the counsellor always to sit in the same place, even if the light varies, and to suggest that the client also should choose, and, if possible, stay with, the same chair. Eye contact may or may not be appropriate. As in any counselling session, regardless of age, the client may turn away when something is difficult to say.

Counselling clients in residential homes can sometimes upset the staff – especially if one introduces painting or modelling, which may be seen as making a mess. Staff can also get suspicious of the counsellor's influence on seemingly docile residents. In one case, a student counsellor was initially welcomed but asked to leave when the residents showed signs of having minds of their own and began questioning staff attitudes.

I have concentrated so far on one-to-one counselling, though I should add that group counselling is often what works best in residential homes, especially for narrative therapy and sharing reminiscences, also for painting, music and drama. Residents and staff in a group together can sometimes be helpful in facilitating mutual understanding, as described by Paul Terry in his book, *Counselling the Elderly and their Carers* (1997).

In groups, clients have an opportunity to help each other and, when this works, there may be a therapeutic boost to self-esteem. 'The group setting can be viewed as akin to a drama where the interaction between group members is a means of acting out personal and collective issues' (McLeod, 1998). A report from Counsel and Care (1994), about depressed old people living at home, focused on groups that started with the intention of helping the bereaved and then expanded according to need. It also described attempts at self-help groups. There was difficulty in defining a homogenous group with differences in age (60–80), men/women, black/white, Jewish/Christian. The advantage was that all could benefit, giving and receiving help without loss of dignity. As old people, they could be senior and respected and not 'talked down to'. But there were also some negative comments. 'Peer counselling can become too friendly. Training is essential.' And, 'I'm not in favour of a peer service – unprofessional, unstructured' (p. 40).

Some vignettes will give an idea of the different settings in which counsellors may find themselves. In the two accounts that follow, I have given some verbatim material to show what actually goes on in sessions – one in the client's home, the other in the counsellor's work room. The first shows how a client's relatives can complicate matters. The second opens up discussion on whether the counsellor was too rigid, and – was she likely to lose this obviously needy client by too strict an observance of rules and time-limits?

Mira

This client did not make the telephone call herself. The call came from her English daughter-in-law, who seemed to have some understanding of the nature of counselling. She explained that Mira was Indian but spoke reasonably good English. 'She's very depressed. The family can do nothing with her.' It happened that a male counsellor lived within walking distance of Mira's home, so he was asked to visit. The door was answered by Ajay, Mira's husband, who introduced himself and then introduced the counsellor to his wife. Clearly, he expected to be present during the session. After an awkward silence, the counsellor addressed Mira. 'It was your daughter-in-law who said she was worried about you, so I've come to see if I can help. If your husband doesn't mind', he glanced at Ajay, 'I'd rather see you alone.' Mira turned from one to the other. It was the first time she had looked up and it was clear that she had been crying. She waited for Ajay to do the talking. 'That would not be suitable,' he said. 'I am not accustomed to allowing my wife to be alone with strangers of the opposite sex. Talk to her by all means, but, as you see, we only have this room. I can be your interpreter – my wife's English is not as good as mine.'

The counsellor turned to Mira, who had not yet spoken. 'Do you understand?' She nodded. 'We could send a female counsellor. In fact, most of our counsellors are women. I'm sorry – we never thought.' He was embarrassed and showed it. It was Ajay who answered him. 'Yes, that would be best. It is what we expected.' The counsellor apologised. 'But she must see you alone,' he said. 'That is what we expect.' Mira didn't speak. Ajay gave a little bow. 'We'd like to help you,' said the counsellor. 'How long have you been in this country?'

Again it was Ajay who replied. 'Thirty years,' he said. 'This is our country. The problem is not with us but with our children. We, the old ones, have changed our nationality, but we are still Hindus. Ours is the oldest religion in the world. But our children have intermarried – my daughter-in-law is a Catholic. She doesn't understand our customs. Yes, Mira will talk to a woman counsellor. Two women together – that would be best.' With another polite bow, Ajay showed the counsellor out. Mira had said nothing.

A female counsellor called. She had lived in India and thought she under-stood Indian customs. This time a granddaughter opened the door. Ajay was out. The girl said she thought the whole family needed counselling. Mira, she said, had been made the scapegoat because she was the most sensitive. 'Wouldn't it be easier if you talked to me?' she suggested. 'I could give you a clearer picture of what's going on.'

'No, I've come to see your grandmother.' The girl shrugged and showed her in. She found Mira unwilling and incoherent. At the end of the hour, she saw the granddaughter again and said she would investigate the possibility of family therapy.

Through contacts, the agency was able to refer the family to a systemic therapist, who was prepared to see the three generations together, listen to their points of view and put their problems in context.

George

This client, from the first telephone call, was fiercely independent and deter-mined to drive himself to the counsellor's work room. He arrived punctu-ally holding a newly lit cigarette. 'Mind if I smoke?' 'Well, yes, actually' was the counsellor's reply. Then, feeling this was inadequate, she suggested he finished his cigarette in the garden. His hand, she saw, was trembling, and, despite an air of bravado, he was plainly nervous. But it didn't occur to her to relax a rule that she had taken for granted would be respected. He was more than five minutes in the garden and she began to wonder if he would re-appear. When he did, she was still obsessed with keeping the rules, which included the convention of the 50 minute hour. 'We have 45 minutes', she told him. 'Do sit down and tell me about yourself.'

'I already have,' he said, 'to the other lady on the phone. Have I got to waste time saying it all again?' Dismayed at having somehow begun the counselling so inauspiciously, she tried to get her thoughts together. 'I know you're not well', she said, 'but I thought it would be more helpful if you told me in your own words.' 'Helpful to who? It's no help to me having to repeat myself.' She saw him get out another cigarette, as though he needed something to hold, but he left it unlit. 'I've got cancer, for God's sake. Cancer of the prostate. They want to give me this hormone treatment.' 'Yes?' 'And I'm going to say no.' She didn't answer, so he went on.

George:	You know what that does? No, I don't suppose you do. It unmans me. That's what it does.
Counsellor:	But — if it saves your life?
George:	What sort of life would that be — only half a man? Worse than being dead — that's what I think.
Counsellor:	You'd still be a person.
George:	Not much of one — not to my way of thinking.

She wanted to let him smoke. How else could he possibly relax? But she felt unable to change the rule that she had so unfortunately laid down. 'You don't understand a thing — never had to cope with cancer, have you?' She winced. 'How can you be so sure?' 'Well, have you?' She wanted to say yes, her husband had died of it, that he smoked himself to death — cancer of the lung. But she kept quiet. 'Then, you can't help me. Nobody can.'

'I'd like to,' she said, 'really I would. Do come again and tell me how you feel. I'd say it needs talking about — whether to have the treatment or not. Don't make hasty decisions. Listen to the doctor.' She felt she was begging him not to leave, that she didn't want to fail him. He was blinking, too proud to cry. She wondered whether to push the box of tissues towards him, but she respected his pride. Men of his generation, she decided, would be ashamed to cry, especially in front of a woman. It also occured to her that men of his generation expected to be allowed to smoke. She thought of all those old movies, in which people kept lighting up. Perhaps next time she would have an ashtray handy — ask her supervisor about that — but perhaps, she thought sadly, there wasn't going to be a next time.

'I'll think about it,' he said. 'I'm sure you mean well, but I'm blessed if I can see what good it will do. No offence meant — you're a good girl.' He shook her hand and she didn't try to stop him. After he had gone, it was she who reached for the tissues.

Assessment and supervision

These two examples show how easily things can go wrong, and the urgent need for supervision. Many services also have an assessment process, whereby each client, before being assigned to a particular counsellor, is given an 'intake' interview by a supervisor or manager, whose job it is to try and 'match' the therapeutic couple, and perhaps make a contract with the client for a commitment of up to six sessions, or some such trial period — though without giving the impression that it is the client who is on trial.

This may be the time – if the service is one that relies on donations to help with the counsellor's expenses – to raise the always uncomfortable question of payment. With these management issues decided beforehand, it could be argued that client and counsellor know where they stand and can get on with the real work that they need to do together. But it can also be argued that contract and money are so important in themselves that they will affect the ongoing client/counsellor relationship. A rapport is often established with the person who takes the first interview, and to whom the client has already unburdened himself, and there may be subsequent disappointment at having to begin again with a stranger. In psychodynamic terminology, it is 'transference' that develops, often starting at the first meeting, with the counsellor representing a parental or authoritative figure, loved or hated in the client's life. Other models use a different language, but acknowledge the importance of the client/counselling relationship in effecting change.

Regular supervision, as every counsellor learns, is a requirement of all professional institutions involved in counselling practice. Not only during training but all through their working lives, counsellors are expected to be supervised by qualified practitioners, more experienced than themselves. There are now special courses to reinforce standards, and from which future supervisors may have to graduate in order to be employed in this capacity. Supervisees also need to learn how to present their case material, either one-to-one with the supervisor, or taking turns in a group, learning from each other's cases and being encouraged to enter into discussion about the issues raised. In the field of old-age counselling, we are all, counsellors and supervisors alike, to some extent, pioneers, learning together and exchanging ideas about what kind of counselling is most effective with an older age group. This is probably best done in groups with, ideally, the supervisor being also available to give individual counsellors support in emergencies, or in strongly emotive situations, such as a client's death.

Hawkins and Shohet (1989) have identified three main functions of supervision in counselling. The first is educational, the aim being to promote theoretical insights. The second is supportive, a sharing of dilemmas and emotions evoked by intense situations with clients. The third is to do with management issues and how to plan the counselling case load.

Supervisors will vary in how they like counsellors to present their material, some wanting detailed verbatim reports, so that each phrase or word can be scrutinised for possible hidden meanings. Others will prefer an overall view of how the counsellor understands the sessions. My own preference is for some verbatim material given in the wider context of how the counselling proceeds from one week to the next. It is usually quite difficult to persuade the counsellor to remember the exact words used in his or her interventions, as more important than those used by the client, and that this is the verbatim that the supervisor needs to hear in order to judge what progress the counsellor is making. As students, counsellors are often asked, with the client's permission, to make tape recordings of sessions. A difficulty here is that the client may feel obliged to comply, even though doing so unwillingly. I would personally feel uncomfortable about asking counsellors to make recordings in the case of elderly clients, who may be unaccustomed to modern technology and highly suspicious of such contrivances, even though they may find it hard actually to say no.

In supervision, or in a special self-awareness group, counsellors can be encouraged to explore any fears or prejudices they may have about their own ageing and how the ageing of others affects them. This may work best in peer support groups, rather than taking up valuable supervision time, but the supervisor, as a trusted 'elder' – even if not older in years – may still have a crucial supporting role.

An important element in supervision is the supervisor's ability to be at one remove from a distressing situation and to hold an objective view, yet without loss of empathy with the counsellor's predicament. The supervisor needs to respect her counsellors as mature people and not to regard her job as telling them what to do, but to get a dialogue going and to respond to the reactions of all the group members to the material presented. She is there to support counsellors when they feel frustrated and stuck, or fearful that the physically frail client might die, or the depressed client give up in despair. The supervisor also advises on questions of management, for instance if and when other authorities should be consulted on the client's state of physical or mental health.

It may be helpful to imagine how supervision would go in the case of the two clients described – Mira and George. In neither case, it seems, was any care taken in matching counsellor to client. In the case of Mira, the client was taken on in response to a third party call and no suggestion made that Mira should make the call herself, or any query about whether she was the family member most in need of counselling. The counsellor was chosen on the grounds of living in the same neighbourhood as the client, although this is often considered a disadvantage, as the client may turn out to have no respect for boundary issues. The service had been alerted to the fact that the client was Indian but there appears to have been no discussion about possible cultural differences. One of the female counsellors had lived in India. Why was she not allocated in the first place? With hindsight, the group might decide that this was a referral that should never have been accepted, or certainly not without consultation. The group turned out to have relevant contacts and the re-referral for family therapy may have rescued the situation. At least those involved in the initial fiasco had the sense to realise the limits of their capabilities and point the Indian family in the direction of a more appropriate resource. Apart from management, there were no supervision issues to address, since the counselling never got started.

In the case of George, there is more to say. Again there was a mismatch. Those responsible for allocating the counsellor knew that the client had cancer. It had already been talked about on the telephone. Probably, somebody in the group knew how the counsellor's husband had died. Or perhaps she should have been wise enough to rule herself out. Smoking was an emotive issue that could not have been foreseen, but, like the cancer, was something she found impossible to look at objectively. Her extreme anxiety, about conforming to what she regarded as commandments set in stone, may have been her way of defending herself against the client's, as well as her own, fear of dying. There was also her fear of failure. She found herself begging him to stay. She could not rescue her husband. Here was another life to be saved. And yet her rigidity was driving him away.

There was much for a supervisor to criticise, for instance the way the counsellor tended to argue with her client rather than tuning in to his actual feelings. Then there was her unswerving obedience to correct counselling behaviour and letting it get in the way of spontaneous response to her client. On the other hand, the supervisor should be aware that this counsellor was clearly a person in need of maximum support to help her through her mourning. This was a case where it would probably be more therapeutic for all concerned if she could allow herself to let go of this client, who might, if he still wanted to come, get more help from a male counsellor, particularly regarding his fear of losing his virility through hormone treatment. As I have already mentioned, compassion is arguably more important than theory, though both qualities are vital if counselling is to be effective.

Reflection and review

- In our dealings with an older generation, it is important to have a sense of history and to take into account the many significant changes that took place in the 20th century. Listening to old people's stories will give some idea of how they coped with the upheavals of two world wars plus a social and sexual revolution. Can you give them credit for their resilience and also be genuinely compassionate if some of them have failed to keep up with the rate of change?
- Do you enjoy listening to old people's memories?
- How much do you know about the hardships affecting ordinary people's lives in the second World War?
- Among your older relatives, at what age did you think of them as becoming old? What characteristics do you associate with old-age?
- What sort of life-experience do you think would most help a counsellor working with older clients?
- Think about your experiences of supervision. What method suits you best – and why?
- What aids do you use for remembering client material – detailed case notes, a few key words and phrases, or do you want to rely on tape recording? Does writing process notes facilitate your own understanding of the main theme in a session?
- What is your understanding of the term 'practice-led theory'?

3

Theory and Practice

I have already, in the last chapter, come out in favour of practice-led theory, but need to expand that concept in order to pinpoint, as far as possible, the place of theory in counselling. The phrase 'to sit lightly' on theory does not mean to dispense with it altogether, but to integrate what we can of textbook words and make them our own. Theory, accepted and understood, will then produce its own language, one that is meaningful to client and counsellor alike. Common sense alone is not enough, even though research that compares the results of professional and lay therapy has often shown the amateur and the trained professional as equally successful. In trying to sift through a babel of different voices, we need to remember that all those theories that have persisted and been handed down have originally been based on therapeutic experiences.

Counselling, these days, is often described as a 'growth industry'. This growth is recent and our older clients may be quite unfamiliar with what counselling actually is. In the beginning was psychoanalysis. It has been with us for a hundred years, so our elders may have grown up with a vocabulary that includes such abstractions as the 'ego' and perhaps the 'id', with the 'unconscious' as a noun, and possibly a hint of what it means to 'repress' and 'resist'. But the expensive and time-consuming process of being analysed was surely not meant for so-called 'ordinary' people.

As practitioners, we may have been trained in one model only; that is the purist view. But, increasingly, counselling trainings have professed to be eclectic, or, more often, integrative, with the emphasis not so much on choosing ideas from a range of theories (eclecticism) but on bringing together a blend of theoretical concepts and trying them out pragmatically with clients in particular situations. Integrationism has been seen (Polkinhorne, 1992) as consistent with our fragmented postmodern society.

With integrationism in mind, it may be useful to look at some of the main counselling models to see what they have to offer our older clients.

Psychodynamic

This is an important element in most integrative training courses, giving a developmental framework which enables the counsellor to take into account each stage of a client's life, in terms of emotional growth or regression. Thus, for instance, a 70 year-old, who presents as over-anxious and dependent, may be exhibiting behaviour which becomes understandable when we learn of her evacuation and extreme home-sickness as a child in the second World War.

Freud set out his developmental programme in psychosexual terms, from infancy to genital maturity. Erikson's eight stages cover the whole of life from birth to death, in a series of opposite possibilities, each needing to be negotiated before moving on. The most relevant in this context is his last stage, 'Integrity versus Despair', and his perceptive conclusion that 'Healthy children will not fear life if their elders have integrity enough not to fear death' (Erikson, 1974: 251).

In the psychodynamic model, there is a strong emphasis on early life affecting the present. Old people, whose distant memories are often clearer than those of more recent times, may be helped by making connections between then and now, and by being enabled to make sense of past conflicts before letting them go.

Object relations theorists developed Freud's ideas by giving importance to relationships, internal as well as external, and especially to mother/child interactions and their lasting effect (as examined by D.W. Winnicott). Earlier relationships are seen to influence that of counsellor and client in the present situation, with the crucial working through of transference, positive and negative. A lot of jargon surrounds these concepts and counsellors need to find appropriate words to be in tune with a client's lifestyle and manner of communication.

The Jungian approach is psychodynamic in that practitioners work with unconscious processes, especially with dreams and what they call 'active imagination', which they see as a way of developing a dream or fantasy in waking life. Jung was particularly interested in life's later stages and in a person's spiritual development. In terms of human progress, older people are seen as striving to realise their potential by discovering a greater self than the conscious ego. This striving is called 'individuation'. Counsellors tend to absorb Jungian ideas through transpersonal trainings, which give the same importance to spirituality. Assagioli's 'psychosynthesis' is the best known of these models.

Humanistic

Carl Rogers' life and work covered most of the 20th century. Under the broader heading of humanistic, his contribution of 'client-centred' or 'non-directive' therapy became widely used, first in America and then in the rest of the world, as a significant alternative to psychoanalysis. It was Rogers who dropped the word 'patient' in favour of 'client', as part of his protest against medical labels, as well as being against analysis and interpretation. His focus was on the counsellor/client relationship, not in terms of transference and countertransference, but as based on unconditional love and trust. He was less concerned with theory than he was with persons, as beings who have two primary needs – for self-actualisation and for love. A client, in Rogers' own words, can be fully functioning if:

> he is able to experience all his feelings, and is afraid of none of his feelings. He is his own sifter of evidence, but is open to evidence from all sources; he is completely engaged in the process of being and becoming himself … he lives completely in this moment, but learns that this is the soundest living for all time. (Rogers, 1963: 22)

It is the task of the counsellor to create the best possible conditions for the client's 'self-process', which is never static, always in a state of becoming. It is the client who, once he can own his feelings and define his ideals, already has the solutions to his difficulties, and can work these out in the presence of a counsellor, whose main contribution is unconditional positive regard.

I can see value for older clients in this Rogerian climate of respect and belief in their capacity for further growth. The immediacy of the present moment, enhanced by speaking in the present tense, encourages release from what may be a burdensome past.

Gestalt psychology comes under the humanistic umbrella, with its central idea that human lives are constantly evolving. When the flow of creative living is dammed up or becomes stereotyped, we become incapable of adapting to new situations and fall back on obsolete responses to what is happening in the here and now. Each gestalt is a temporary configuration of human experience that forms and then dissolves. In each new situation, there is a build-up of interest and energy which lasts as long as there is a need to cope with what is happening and then dissipates as the task is completed and other priorities emerge.

> The emerging and receding of different gestalts is a continuous process. If interrupted, the gestalt may not complete its life-cyle … Unfulfilled states of being result from such interruptions, many of which are self-induced or repetitive. (Parlett and Hemming, 1996: 199)

It is a therapy that, not unlike Zen meditation, increases our awareness of the present moment and opens us to new experience.

I can see value in these conceptions when working with elderly people. We may be able to help them confront each new trauma of loss or disability, as well as new ways of having to live – for instance, in sheltered accommodation – ways which are not of their choosing but offer a different, and perhaps, challenging mode of being in the world. Awareness of the changing body, recognising feelings and sensations, will keep the old person in touch with what is real, not only with that which has been lost, but also with that which still feels good. This emphasis on the body is not on its medical shortcomings but on feelings of aliveness that persist despite disability and pain. Humanistic counsellors often use gestalt techniques, which, at their most creative, feel to the participant like playing interesting games, as well as releasing pent-up emotions and learning to relax. These games will include dialogue between different parts of the self, working with dreams, visualisation, painting and physical movement.

have all (whether in personal therapy or experiential groups) had experience in self-exploration. They have also been supervised, and discussed a range of counselling skills.

In my experience, I have found that, at their best, counsellors move easily and sensitively from one mode of working to another, as I think the following illustration exemplifies. I include it here in the counsellor's own words.

Case study – 'M'

For the past 13 years, I have worked as a chiropodist with predominantly older patients, so I am well accustomed to the elderly. I was, however, anticipating moving in my work as a counsellor to a younger age group and it was my belief that anyone over 65 could not respond to counselling because of being unwilling to change. I had been told so many times, 'you can't teach an old dog new tricks', that I believed this was the general view of the elderly. I was convinced that my view was accurate and would not have considered myself prejudiced. My blinkers were removed when I was asked to visit a 76 year-old woman as a counsellor. At first I refused, saying I did not counsel the elderly, but the matron of the nursing home was desperate, as she had tried in vain to help this resident. Because I was impressed by this forward-thinking, caring matron, I agreed to see the old lady, but I still insisted that I probably would not be able to help.

My first impression of M was of a very weak, depressed old lady. She was sitting, propped up in a chair, her left leg hanging helplessly over a foot-stool, her corresponding arm lying uselessly on a pillow over her knee. Her mouth was drooped slightly, making her speech a little slurred. She was the victim of a cerebral vascular accident (CVA), commonly known as a stroke. In that first session, I listened to her story and I struggled with my preconceived ideas and my desire to help. At the end of the session, M said to me desperately, 'please will you help me. I don't mind what I do. I'll do whatever you want me to, if I can get better.'

I knew I could not refuse her, and I also knew that I had been invested with tremendous power both from the matron and the client. I could use this power to enable and empower her or to keep her dependent and disempowered. I needed to take a long look at my own attitudes regarding the elderly and this client in particular ... Even in the excellent home, my client's needs can only be partly met. The staff are frequently too busy, too few or too young and inexperienced to have awareness of the deep needs of an elderly person in their care, the need to treat each one as a unique, valuable individual, instead of one of fifty others who have to be washed, dressed and sitting in their chairs by coffee time. There is no time to allow the elderly stroke victims to carry out minor tasks slowly and laboriously, nor is there time to supervise, support or sit and listen for a while. This situation creates an ambivalence. Part of the person wants to be a 'good patient', who makes no demands, so that 'they' will like her and treat her kindly. But another, needier, part cries out for her needs to be met and knows that if she doesn't make demands, she will be ignored. Thus the staff have power over her, and, when she hears them talking outside her door about not answering another resident's bell because 'she only wants to chat', her vulnerability and powerlessness is increased …

At the first session, we were interrupted twice by staff, bustling in and out, for unnecessary reasons. This made me angry as I had requested that we should be undisturbed. I asked M how she felt about such intrusion and she admitted that she hated it, but that they always did it, even when the vicar came. I made a point of seeing Matron about this and explained the importance of privacy. Consequently, from then on, a 'DO NOT DISTURB' notice was kept in the room and at each session I pinned it on the door. M commented that her time with me was the only time when she was allowed any privacy. She explained how she had been left sitting on the toilet with the door open while nurses chatted outside. When we talked about this, she expressed feelings of despair at her loss of dignity and independence because of the stroke. In the middle of doing a relaxation exercise with her, the chiropodist burst into the room, informing me that she had to have her feet attended to. I was very aware of my own transference here, but I was more conscious of wanting to protect my client. I told the chiropodist that we were having a therapy session, and pointed out the notice on the door. He went away somewhat reluctantly, and she thanked me, saying this was the kind of situation that happened again and again, and she was powerless to do anything about it.

M then told me about a regular visitor who stayed too long and talked 'at' her about things that upset her. The person in question had been her cleaner before she had the stroke, and had now seemingly taken on the role of 'daughter' or 'friend', a role which M had not given her. As she spoke, M became very agitated about this woman and her patronising way of speaking, telling M such things as, 'you'll soon be back home, digging your garden'. I asked what she would really like to say to her if she could, and she answered, 'I'd say get the hell out of here and never come back!' She then got upset and said she had never wanted to be unkind to anyone before. We explored this feeling of helplessness and being trapped in her chair, at the mercy of whoever wanted to come into the room. I showed her various assertiveness techniques which she practised on me, and I responded in various ways. She found this helpful but still felt powerless with her unwelcome visitor. Some weeks later, I arrived to find her very distressed, as she had asked the staff if they could stop this person coming to see her. They had chided her, like a child, and told her she was 'very naughty' in wanting to be so unkind to this 'wonderful' person who visited her so regularly. She was distraught at feeling so trapped within her body, and helpless against the force of 'caring' people who now controlled her life …

Many elderly people in homes live with the constant frustration of not getting needs met and not daring to challenge what is being put upon them. In my work with M, I used fantasy journeying as well as music, Play-Doh and pictures to help M get in touch with her inner self and discover her own resources. There is a strong transference, with M seeing me as the mother who protects her in her vulnerability.

The outcome of the incident, just described, was encouraging. Initially, M asked if I would talk to the Matron on her behalf, and I willingly did this, having found out exactly how M wanted to be represented. Following our discussion, Matron talked with M and decided with her that all her visitors should report to the staff before seeing her, and this one, in particular, would be told M was not well or able to see her. I was not fully satisfied with this arrangement, but I felt it would work in the short term, and this would give M time to explore what she really wanted to do.

The incident revealed some big underlying issues about how M felt in her newly disabled body, with friends and particularly a 'cleaning woman', who were able-bodied and enjoying a normal life that had been cruelly snatched from her. Much anger and despair surfaced and, through therapy, she was able to recognise and express buried feelings and face the loss which had previously been 'bravely' denied. She then moved on to sad, guilty feelings about her inability to communicate honestly with people. She wanted to put things right, but didn't know how ...

The young staff advised M to 'forget it – if you don't want to see her, why bother?' But she obviously needed to find her way of putting things right. Using a gestalt technique, I enabled M to face R and say what she really wanted to tell her. A few weeks later, she told me delightedly that she had seen R and was able to tell her, calmly and concisely, what she felt. The meeting ended with R hugging M and thanking her for explaining everything. She is now visiting occasionally, according to the boundaries M has set. M felt very satisfied with this, and, with new courage was able to tell some more visitors that she couldn't cope with them all coming at once. They now ring before they come and consider her feelings ...

Endings are a big issue for the elderly, simply because their time on 'this mortal coil' is running out. In a residential nursing home, where friendships are made and ended by death, sometimes on a weekly basis, these endings are yet another burden for the elderly person. I had already worked through a guided fantasy with M saying goodbye to a friend who had died just prior to her stroke, and on letting go of her home, neighbours, cat and past life. M had found this helpful. I was made aware that death was something she dreaded by her reaction to the death of a lady in the next room, who had seemed in better health than herself. M was overwhelmed and deteriorated physically and mentally. I felt she was ready to explore her own death and ending. When I tentatively approached the subject, she was eager to share her fears ...

As a Christian, with a faith that is important to me, it would be easy for me to overpower, rather than empower, her and I explored this fully in supervision before opening up the spiritual area with M. We are still working in this area and the work we have done has been the most moving and enriching that I have ever had the privilege to share with another human being. With close supervision, I have been able to 'be there' for M, holding, as it were, the tips of her fingers, as she makes her journey and reaches out into her unknown. I have often felt, during the guided fantasies, that, if I said anything, I would intrude. So I am standing, watching, as M discovers her own eternal destiny and inner peace ...

Through these sessions, I have observed a great change in M. It is not just the outward change that has turned her from a defeated, crumpled old lady, waiting to die, to the alert, expectant person she is now. This is deeper, a spiritual dimension, where she experiences peace instead of fear and distress, and, more than that, she now has an inner strength and empowerment, where she was so powerless.

In February, when I first visited M, the huge horse chestnut tree outside her window looked bare and dead. M didn't look out of the window much at that time, so, knowing her love of gardening, I thought this might be a useful place to tap her energy sources. I brought a begonia corm in a pot and put it on her window sill, and we explored the cycle of life and growth. The tree outside has now bloomed, and is covered in rich green leaves. The begonia has changed from a dead-looking, earth-bound object to a beautiful plant, cascading with flowers. And M – what of her place in this ongoing cycle of life and growth? I can only quote her words when I saw her last time: 'You know, I thought I was finished when I came here, and I wanted to die. But now I feel as if my life has begun again, and I think I want to live a bit.' (Brotherton, 1995)

From this account, we can see that M's counsellor was able to integrate the counselling models she had studied in her training. It should be helpful to look at these in turn.

Psychodynamically, she was aware of her client's transference as a re-enactment of a helpless infant relationship, with herself, in her counselling role, as the all-powerful adult, who seemed to have the means to bring about the cure that the old lady was so desperately asking for. The counsellor did not, however, encourage the client in an exploration of her early life. The therapy took place in the present tense and particularly with the here-and-now issues of loss and disempowerment, so relevant to M's situation after her stroke.

Humanistically, the counsellor was able, in a Rogerian way, to enable her client to experience feelings that, up to then, had been 'bravely' denied, and this included an expression of anger against an intrusive visitor, with whom M did not want an intimate relationship but felt it was being forced upon her. The counsellor used a gestalt exercise for M to confront this visitor and say what she really wanted to tell her.

By the means of assertiveness techniques, which the client was encouraged to practise with the counsellor, a gradual change developed in the client's behaviour and, more importantly, in the client's view of her behaviour, so that she could begin to challenge the staff when she perceived them as treating her like a naughty, ungrateful child. This cognitive behavioural input helped to raise M's self-esteem, which had been much diminished by being 'trapped in her chair'. Slowly, she could begin to realise that she did not have to be entirely at the mercy of other people's treatment of her, but still had a voice and point of view of her own.

The counsellor also used relaxation exercises, fantasy journeys, music, play and the symbolism of a growing plant. In a transpersonal mode, she was able to add a spiritual dimension, while taking care not to intrude on her client's individual exploration of death and the unknown.

Putting theory into practice is a theme that will be pursued throughout this book, with many illustrations of how both theory and practice can be used with older clients.

Reflection and review

- In the debate between 'pure' and integrative models of therapy, think about where you stand. Can you communicate easily with people who come from a different counselling background?
- What do you think are the advantages of integrationism? Are there any drawbacks?
- The case study in this chapter showed various ways in which a counsellor was able to empower a helpless old lady. Did you feel that the counsellor succeeded in putting theory into practice, through integrating the models of counselling that she had been taught? I suggest you think about your own practice and how far you are able to absorb different theories while developing a style of your own.

4

Time-limited or Open-ended:
Beginning and Ending

In the ongoing debate about the merits of short- or long-term therapy, the case for time-limited seems to be winning. In applying the argument to old-age counselling, I acknowledge the pros and cons of either choice, but only with the proviso that there should be no discrimination in referring older people to time-limited therapy (as 'second best') on account of their age, instead of as a carefully chosen procedure to suit each individual case.

We need to examine how old people experience the passage of time. We see them as having time on their hands, and yet every task, every move, takes longer to accomplish. Sometimes it seems that both energy and time are in short supply. When looking back on youth and childhood, we often hear them say, 'it seems like yesterday', as though no time has passed at all. As young old-age moves into old old-age, short-term memory begins to weaken; stories get repeated; communication slows down. And yet there is nothing inevitable about this slowing. We must constantly remind ourselves that individuals vary in their ageing, and we must prepare for being astonished by wisdom and vitality just as often as we may be disappointed by failing memory.

An article on clearly defined four-session therapy concludes with these words:

> Time as a delimiting factor constitutes a challenge both for the patient and the therapist. It compels an awareness of life's limitations from the first moment of the encounter. At the same time, it accentuates that 'our time is here and now', i.e. the clear and distinct frame serves to intensify the feeling of 'now' and being 'present'. (Fyro, Hardell and Westlund Cederroth, 1999: 465–81)

Therapy as containment, the 'clear and distinct frame', together with emphasis on living in the present, might be seen as offering older people a sense of shape in a shapeless world and 'good moments' (Mahrer et al., 1987) to hold and be held by.

But by time-limited I would hope for 12 or 20 sessions, carefully structured and with the end-date known from the beginning. Anything shorter would, I think, include the possibility of coming back for more 'one day', though not necessarily with the same therapist. In old-age, one might feel that any hoped-for change needs to happen quickly, or not at all. If, on the other hand, the therapy is open-ended, it is probable that the same amount of change will come about, more slowly and perhaps more comfortably, but with the risk of greater dependence, a more painful ending and the client getting lost in a maze of possibilities, instead of experiencing the continuing containment that might have been expected.

We associate long-term therapy with Freudian – and also Jungian – analysis, but it is interesting to note that Freud, as founding father, did not, in fact, go in for those extended courses of treatment practised by those who came after him. A lot, of course, depends on aims, and Freud was famously pessimistic in claiming that all he could realistically achieve was to change 'hysterical misery into common unhappiness' (1895). Other analysts have aimed at transforming a person's entire character structure, and that can take years.

In choosing to work briefly with an older age group, we need to find a focus that is mutually agreed between counsellor and client at the assessment stage, and to determine whether or not the client is able to stay with this focus without wandering in directions not designated for exploration. Choosing and sticking with the chosen focus may turn out to be the most difficult part of the counselling task. If open-ended therapy is an available alternative, the decision whether or not to take on a person for time-limited work needs to be made at this initial session.

Time-limited counselling in action

Mary

Mary was 73, a mother and grandmother whose husband had been diagnosed with Alzheimer's. She was nursing him at home. The focus agreed on with the assessor was her feeling of guilt at finding herself surviving and mentally active while her husband deteriorated. She was afraid that her bouts of anger and impatience would hasten his death. She arrived for her first session, full of resentment, that having told her story to the assessor, she now had to repeat it to another counsellor – what a waste of time. She was to have 15 weekly sessions and a follow-up 6 months later.

The counsellor's preferred model was psychodynamic, though she was also conversant with the Rogerian approach. In practising time-limited therapy, she was influenced by Malan (1976, 1979) and Davanloo (1980). She had been taught to discourage any deep transference relationship, not by denial, but by promptly identifying its onset, and to concentrate on what was happening between counsellor and client in their weekly meetings. She knew that they would both have to work hard in the short time available, and was dismayed that her first session with Mary was so taken up with irritation about the counselling arrangements that she found herself fearful that valuable time was already ebbing away. She felt powerless to seize the moment and find any clear goal for them to work towards. 'You seem a very angry person', was all she could find to say. 'Am I?' said Mary, who seemed at first surprised and then distressed. She burst into tears. 'You make me feel so dreadfully guilty.'

Counsellor:	Why should I do that? [*Silence: Mary continued to sob.*]
Counsellor:	I'm wondering how it was when you were a child, and if you often felt told-off.
Mary:	Of course I did – all the time.
Counsellor:	By your mother?
Mary:	Both of them, but Mother most of all. I was never good enough.
Counsellor:	I'm not your mother.

By the end of the first session, a theme had emerged round the phrase 'not good enough', and, at their next meeting, Mary talked freely about how her husband, always charming and easy-going, had been the first person in her life to love her for herself, instead of trying to turn her into someone else. There arose the question 'Was the counsellor trying to turn her into someone else?' and the repeated reminder 'I'm not your mother'.

There was, predictably, a lot of anguish about her husband's dementia, the loss of his personality and also, it seemed, of his love for her, and how much she had needed him to reflect back to her that she was an attractive and likeable person. Without that reflection, her whole existence seemed threatened. 'I no longer know who I am', said Mary desperately.

Reflective listening of a Rogerian kind seemed to be needed as was also the mirror transference (Kohut and Wolf, 1978) that reflected back to the client a positive sense of self. Anger, and fear of that anger, surfaced again, sometimes with the ferocity of a child's temper tantrum. But, as Mary internalised some of the counsellor's calm acceptance of her moods, she became able to tolerate the ambivalent feelings she now experienced towards her previously 'perfect' husband, and to relinquish some of that urgent need for reparation that had driven her to be his sole carer, giving herself no pause or rest. The counsellor asked her who she was trying to appease, and, with sudden insight, Mary recognised that it was her critical parents, long since dead. The counsellor asked her about her two sons. One lived and worked in Australia. The other urged her to put his father in a home and look after herself.

Counsellor:	Have you discussed that solution with him?
Mary [*vehemently*]:	How could I? That would be to lose my husband altogether.
Counsellor:	But aren't you losing him already?

At first Mary was obstinate, refusing to face the reality of the dementia which would gradually distance him so far from her that communication between them would cease. She had been taking refuge up till now in her obsessive care, shutting off her thoughts and feelings through the practical chores which tired her out so that she felt numb, but still insisted that this was what she, and she alone, must do for him. The counsellor was ruthless in presenting her with a realistic picture of her husband's future, while, at the same time, continuing to reflect back to her the image of a capable and still energetic self, who was temporarily worn down by too much strenuous physical work. She also reminded Mary of her age. It turned out that both her sons had said much the same but Mary had refused to listen. She was listening now, and, as the counselling neared its end, was able, without guilt, to admit that she was weak and tired and perhaps, for her sons' sake, should think of her own future, because she didn't want to be a burden to them. 'Not just for their sake', said the counsellor. 'What about your own happiness?' Mary shrugged that off – as if she couldn't believe anyone cared. But soon after this session, she got in touch with her local branch of the Alzheimers' Disease Society and was able to accept what respite care they were able to give her.

The sessions had to end. Mary couldn't say goodbye without tears, but was comforted by the counsellor's evident faith in her strength. The counsellor had reservations – she would have liked to work with Mary for longer – but the six month follow-up showed a stronger, healthier Mary. Her husband had settled surprisingly easily into a residential home and Mary now lived in a bungalow next door to her second son. She found herself welcomed by her grandchildren, who had encouraged her to buy a computer and were amused and delighted by her efforts to master the mysteries of the internet. She could now send e-mails to her son in Australia, and marvelled at the wonders of technology that closed the gap between them. She still had twinges of survivor guilt and real sadness every time she visited her husband, but she was at last managing to separate his life from hers. In the continuing family of her sons and grandchildren, she was feeling loved and valued.

Despite her counsellor's early doubts, Mary's therapy achieved the goals decided at the assessment stage. Guilt was greatly diminished, links having been made with figures from the past. Anger and frustration were seen as resulting from the non-recognition which had dogged her early years, and been painfully reactivated by her husband's Alzheimer's. The counsellor was able to break through the 'bad' mother transference instead of allowing it to grow, and, with similar assertiveness, to attack Mary's obsessive nurturing behaviour and show her that it was performed as much to prove her own goodness – to her dead parents and to herself – as for her husband's well-being. Time being too short for sitting back and waiting for Mary to understand and work through her defences against facing the sadness of what had happened to her marriage, she had to be confronted with painful truths, while, at the same time being recognised as strong enough to cope with them. A new-found confidence in her own strength released Mary from clinging to a hopelessly stuck position, so that she could move closer to the healthy family that was left to her, and whose appreciation she could enjoy. Long-term therapy might have given her more insight but, even in the few months alloted to her, she seems to have gained as much as she needed. It could be argued that her sense of identity was still so flimsy that it needed propping up by others, and that more work could have been done to foster self-reliance. On the other hand, she was approaching a time in her life at which independence has gradually to be surrendered, and help from willing others accepted rather than uselessly fought against.

In Rogerian language, what made a difference in Mary's therapy had less to do with transference from past relationships than the counsellor's empathy, congruence and 'unconditional positive regard'. Where Freud could only hope for a state of common unhappiness, Rogers had faith in a person's intrinsic goodness and capacity for self-actualisation, provided he or she could be given value by another human being. In the absence of pathology, there is no need to talk about 'cure' or even the removal of symptoms. Whatever the counsellor's theoretical position, it was certainly possible, in Mary's case, to fulfil the modest aim of making enough difference for this client to move out of her obsessive role of one and only carer, so that she could reach a stage of being able (again I quote Freud) 'to love and to work' – even though she was far past the age when he would have accepted her for therapy!

Some difficulties

Time-limited therapy, we have to remember, is not always undertaken out of choice but more often from necessity. I have already argued (Orbach, 1996) that, given time and money, older people should have as much right as the young to long-term, or open-ended, treatment. Most older people, however, have stopped earning. Their pensions are often inadequate and they are reluctant to spend their savings. For many, the obvious place to take their troubles, whether physical, emotional, or both, is to the GP's surgery. The doctor, with a queue of patients in his waiting room, has only a short time to listen, so, unless the patient shows bizarre behaviour, the only treatment immediately available is the giving out of sleeping pills and anti-depressant drugs; or – and this is increasingly likely – the possibility of brief therapy with a counsellor employed by the surgery.

The limit is usually 12 sessions, though, if this proves obviously inadequate, a further series can sometimes be arranged. The client (or, in this context, the patient) having been referred by a doctor, may be imbued with the idea of having an illness, for which pills have been prescribed – and how can mere talking bring about a cure? It may take nearly half the permitted sessions to overcome suspicion of what is seen by the client as a 'last resort', a way of softening the blow of being pronounced incurable. Of course, the experience is not always as bad as that, but it can be quite difficult to break through the medical model. The doctor has perhaps given his elderly patient only a hazy account of what to expect from counselling; he may be unconvinced himself of its effectiveness and possibly he did make the referral as a last resort and because he was reluctant to dose his patient with stronger drugs, knowing them to be addictive and to have side-effects.

At best, doctor and counsellor have regular meetings to discuss the patients from their different points of view and learn about their separate disciplines, but it frequently turns out that both are too busy for this useful contact. When the initial assessment is made by a doctor, the result is, more than likely, couched in terms of a diagnosis. This patient is suffering from depression, from post-traumatic-syndrome, or from bereavement, as though that too is an illness.

Another difficulty is the 'presenting problem', which the counsellor has learnt to regard as superficial and masking a deeper trouble. A trained assessor would be on the watch to catch at least some hint of what is hidden, and whether time-limited therapy is the appropriate response. But, faced with only 12 sessions, the counsellor may have little opportunity to explore beyond what is first presented. Spacing the sessions with more than the usual weekly intervals may or may not be helpful. The disadvantage could be that the all-important counsellor/client contact becomes too tenuous.

Open-ended counselling

Counselling is seldom as long-term as analytic psychotherapy, but, despite the current trend towards brief interventions, and the cogent arguments in favour of a finite series of sessions, agreed from the beginning, I have doubts about whether short-term work should be our standard response to the problems of old age.

My experience in this field has shown me that old people are inclined to be slow in getting started. They are entering what, to a lot of them, is unfamiliar territory, and it has been a hard decision to open up to a stranger. It seems to me that it is up to us, as counsellors, to put them at their ease and not to hurry them. Giving the process more time does not mean that we are expecting to produce a magic cure, nor is it our job to equip these clients for any obvious success in a future that is gradually, or perhaps quite rapidly, shrinking. The emphasis will be on the past and the need to come to terms with events that cannot be changed. There is often a need to forgive other people and themselves for quarrels and misunderstandings, the letting go of unproductive bitterness and generally making sense of their life stories. Listening to stories takes time, but, as we will see in the next chapter, being able to tell, and re-tell, them to an attentive listener can be an essential therapeutic task. There is value in coasting along at the old person's pace. Listening to repetitions, we should not dismiss what we hear as mindless rambling, but respect the urgency behind what the client is trying to express.

One of the difficulties in time-limited therapy, as already mentioned, is the masking of deep-seated conflict by what has come to be known as the 'presenting problem' and its non-emergence in the initial assessment, as illustrated by the following case study.

Bob

Bob came into counselling in his mid 70s. He was a flood victim, who had been given temporary accommodation while the damage to his home was assessed and arrangements made for the cleaning up of the house. He was shaken by what had happened and disorientated by the sudden move. He said he needed help in making up his mind about whether to move from an isolated village into the nearest town. He was still driving but anxious about main roads and roundabouts. Perhaps he should live in a place where he did-n't need a car. But he loved the country and so did his old dog, who was his only companion. Anxiety about what to do was affecting his sleep. This was the problem presented and neither Bob, nor his counsellor, expected his counselling to last long. He came once a week and no end-date was fixed.

Talking about his insomnia, Bob showed signs of embarrassment and was unable to look his counsellor in the face. There was an awkward silence and the counsellor remarked on his heavy breathing.

Bob:	Please, please – don't use that word.
Counsellor [puzzled]:	Which word?
Bob:	I c-can't say it – [in a whisper] 'breathing'.
Counsellor:	But – it's so vital to life. I can't promise never to mention it.
Bob:	I usually keep this secret – but, if I tell you, please try to understand. You see – insomnia isn't quite the right word. I'll try and explain.

He described feelings of panic when he woke each morning and it seemed that the passage from sleeping to waking was frightening. He found it hard to make the transition from consciousness to sleep, hard to let go. But it was even harder to wake in the mornings. His mother, with whom he had not lived for long, had given him a rag to hold on to, and he was ashamed to admit that he still needed that rag, though it was full of holes from chewing it.

Counsellor:	Chewing it?
Bob:	I'm so frightened, you see. Mum gave it to me to stop me spoiling the sheets.
Counsellor:	You never lived with her for long. Perhaps the rag reminds you of her.
Bob [surprised]:	Then, why chew it?
Counsellor:	More like – kissing?

Bob shook his head. She never kissed him. Instead of saying more about his mother, Bob told the story of his wife's death from lung cancer. He had looked after her, but had not been in the room when she died, 'when she,' he whispered, 'took her last breath'. He had been walking the dog. Perhaps just as well, he said, because he didn't like transitions.

When he at last got going, Bob had a confusing story to tell. His mother was married to Mr Jones, whose name he had been given, but he lived most of the time with Mr Smith and a motherly housekeeper. When he married, he overheard something his mother was saying to his wife: 'Be careful – just one little slip and you're landed with it'. What could she mean? He went on to say that he had never been much good at sex. Then he got embarrassed but somehow managed to convey that foreplay was pleasurable though intercourse had always been a problem, and this was hard on his wife who had wanted children. He associated intercourse with heavy breathing (he stumbled over the word) and getting out of control. He became tearful and ashamed, calling himself a failure. His counsellor, noticing that he had managed to talk about sex and use the forbidden word 'breathing', decided to keep him at it. She said she wondered whether his sense of failure had something to do with that remark of his mother's and her admonition to be careful, presumably about birth control and unwanted pregnancies. He seemed not to listen. Then, very sadly, he said, 'Perhaps Mum never wanted me'.

At the time of his marriage, Bob had written to Mr Jones asking if there was something about his birth that he had not been told. The reply was, 'Look at your birth certificate. You'll find it quite in order.' And his mother had added that he was lucky – some people might envy a birth certificate like that.

He showed his counsellor photos of Mr Jones and Mr Smith. 'Which do I look like?' The photos were old and blurred and she couldn't see any obvious likeness. 'What do you think?' she asked. It was clear that he thought Mr Smith (with whom he had lived) was his father. But he wanted that confirmed. 'Why couldn't they tell me the truth?' He had been agonising for years over the uncertainty. Both Jones and Smith were long since dead, and so was his mother. There would never be absolute proof. Yet, during his time with the counsellor, he became slowly convinced that he had worked out the truth for himself – that he was sure, and he thought his counsellor was sure (though she never said so), that Mr Smith was his father.

But he still minded that his mother had never been straight with him. There were more tears to shed and his counsellor stayed with him in his mourning. It was Bob who suggested they might end soon because he had got what he needed from counselling. He weaned himself very gradually, admitting that he had looked forward to the sessions as bringing some warmth in an empty life. By this time, he had moved from country to town, but still yearned for the country. He still had the rheumatic old dog for company, and taking country walks was one of his chief pleasures, though now he needed the car to reach the country and his favourite walks. The counsellor feared that he would soon have another death. Already he could outwalk the dog.

Bob cut his sessions from weekly to fortnightly, then once a month. Eventually he thought he could manage on his own. He determinedly said goodbye, knowing he could come back if he felt the need. But he never did.

In Bob's case, the presenting problem was less satisfactorily cleared up than his phobia about breathing, and the secrets in his life that had caused it. He was given as much time as he wanted – more than a year – and allowed to end when he felt ready. A cognitive behavioural approach might have coped in a shorter time with his phobia, but, most probably, he would never have discovered the cause, nor would he have unravelled the family secret that had worried him right through his life. Bob was lucky in being able to pay a modest fee for his counselling.

Endings

Beginnings can be controversial – do we just plunge in or do we make careful assessments? I think most of us are in favour of the latter and that the end should be built into the beginning, especially in time-limited work. Endings, in my opinion, ought to be discussed in far more depth than they usually are, both on training courses and in supervision. And whose decision should it be to wind things up – the counsellor's, the client's or by mutual consent? In time-limited work, the problem is solved. The client gives consent to the limit before the therapy begins.

> Managing endings without acting out and spotting the moment when it is possible for both participants to let go and say goodbye is surely one of the most important therapeutic skills. (Mander, 2000: 301–17)

Many practitioners agree that therapy has a way of ending either too late or too soon. If the ending is mishandled, both counsellor and client are affected. Sometimes a premature ending comes about for reasons no one can control – sudden crises, deaths in the family or unforeseen geographical moves. In such cases a re-referral seems to be the only answer, but may prove an unsatisfactory solution if the therapy is going well and the client/counsellor relationship well established. In such a case, there is too much to mourn so quickly. If the therapy has not been going well, the client may be too disenchanted to face starting again. In the absence of a time-limited contract, it may be impossible to choose the exact moment of readiness. Bob, as just described, clearly thought that he had, and never asked for a follow-up. So the counsellor is left not knowing, but hoping that, together, they got the timing right. The impression is that this client was able to shake himself free of dependency and recognise his separate existence. Like many older people, he was used to being alone and could manage a certain stoicism when faced with loneliness. To expect a perfect ending is, of course, as unrealistic as hankering after a mythical paradise. Separating from loved and important figures never happens at a guaranteed time, and old age, as we know, is full of mourning. Ending therapy can be seen as a rehearsal for death. But the loss need not be sudden and the mourning period can be begun while the therapy is still a living experience. Thus an unthinkable end may become bearable and the client emerge from it better prepared for the deaths, sudden or prolonged, that are bound to accumulate as he grows older, culminating, of course, with his own.

Others, if therapy is open-ended, may try hard to avoid the inevitable end. Sometimes, with old people, there is an actual forgetting (either deliberate or unconscious) of the planned date. An 87 year-old arrived for her last session in a state of anxiety at having left her diary at home. 'But we don't need diaries', said her therapist. There was a long pause, till at last she admitted, 'Yes, I know, but I'm wriggling.' An elderly male client, with a life-story as complicated as Bob's, had to be let down by his counsellor because she became ill and had to give up work. So another female counsellor took her place and he coped surprisingly well with this change – one of the complications of his story having been that he was brought up by two mothers. His dependency was not on a particular person but on the counselling service that supplied them. However, his third and final counsellor was a man, and this different experience broke the pattern and eventually helped him to end.

It is obviously too simplistic to say that readiness to end comes when the assessment goals have been achieved. In Mary's case, that was what happened. With others, whether the therapy is time-limited or left open, more problems arise in the course of working with what has been presented. Avoiding what comes up is not always an option. All the counsellor can hope to do is build up confidence and perhaps indicate possible ways of coping without therapeutic help. But this may not satisfy the client.

One could argue that ageing clients are not going to be re-born and make their mark on the world as a result of being counselled. Yet sometimes they may emerge with a few new insights, awareness of choices, however small, that can improve the quality of their lives, and even, perhaps, a hint of serenity before they die. These are the hopes we hold for them and hopes can sometimes be infectious.

Reflection and review

- Think about the advantages and disadvantages of time-limited counselling. How many sessions do you think you would need for brief therapy with an elderly person?
- What ideas have you on determining counselling aims and how flexible do you think you could be on discovering that your client has a different agenda?
- What, generally speaking, are your criteria for ending a course of counselling?
- Freud is reported to have said, 'Once the therapist has fixed the time-limit, he cannot extend it, otherwise the patient would lose all faith in him'. Do you agree with this statement or would you prefer less rigidity?
- What do you think about 'keeping the door open' after ending with a client in case he needs to return?

5

The Use and Value of Stories

> We are all tellers of tales. We each seek to provide our scattered and often confusing experiences with a sense of coherence by arranging the episodes of our lives into stories … Through our personal myth, each of us discovers what is true and meaningful in life. (McAdams, 1993: 11)

This personal myth is something which we build gradually throughout our lives. It is not mere myth, a fairy story that is untrue, but the meaning we give to the factual happenings that we pass through. Facts may get forgotten but meanings can develop and change over the years.

The old are archetypal story-tellers. Traditionally, they have handed on the history of the tribe. This is a role that seems to have got lost in today's postmodern culture with its denial of fixed meanings and fragmentation of communal experience. Instead of stories being embedded in one tradition, we are now bombarded, through the technological revolution, by a seemingly unlimited choice of stories from all times and all places. It is hard, in this global situation, especially for older people, to value the wisdom they might hope to have attained through their individual life-time experiences, especially when children and grandchildren do not want to listen to their 'old-fashioned' stories.

The attitude of the counsellor to reminiscence, personal myth, the healing power of stories and a wide range of narrative therapies is what I intend to explore in this chapter.

Reminiscence

There has been an attitude among professional carers that reminiscing should be discouraged on the grounds that it is not good for old people to 'live in the past', as if today's reality were more important than the story-making of a life-time. Fortunately times are changing, and 'reminiscence work', often in groups, has come to be seen as effective in reducing anxiety and building up positive images of the self. The term 'reminiscence therapy' is sometimes used interchangeably with 'life review therapy'. Other researchers (Lashley, 1993, Haight and Burnside, 1993) see each as a different therapeutic approach, with some specialised training required for practising life review, as a more in-depth process, than a straightforward disclosure of memories. Reminiscence work encourages positive remembering, and can be practised by carers, nurses, occupational therapists and all those involved in day-to-day communication with old people. The skills needed are active listening, empathy and a genuine interest in both the client and the client's history, all of them basic counselling skills which facilitators should be encouraged to learn.

A reminiscence group gives isolated old people, living alone, a chance to socialise, and could be a useful adjunct to a day centre. Old people in residential care may be just as lonely and shut in on themselves as those in their own homes, and a group of this kind can be beneficial in fostering friendships among residents, through the sharing of memories. Facilitators need to be careful about who to include and wary of those who show paranoid behaviour, as well as some of those who persist in being reticent about exposing personal feelings. Too much probing, especially by unqualified helpers, should be avoided. The group is there for support and the building of self-esteem, not for painful disclosure.

However much we associate ageing with memory loss (which no one can deny), when it comes to old people telling their stories, we find that major life events, such as births, deaths, marriages, illnesses or war, are usually recalled with a fair amount of accuracy. Distortions often have to do with fitting remembered details into a person's existing mental schema, as part of an overall making sense of what has now become history, and integrating it with present experience. We each of us have pictures of incidents, places and people in our individual past, like collections of photographs in family albums, to which we keep returning. They may not be historically accurate – forgotten details have been replaced by imaginative embellishments – but these pictures are essential to the forming of our individual scripts. In the confusion of dementia, people can no longer tell their stories, so it is hard to know, from outside, how many of the pictures get lost. There is no order in them as collections, though it seems that there are occasional glimpses, out of sequence but still vivid, which are important to their owners, and this should be recognised by the friends or counsellors to whom they may be shown. Communication, including counselling, with dementing clients is something that I shall try to address in a later chapter.

Life review

A spontaneous urge to make sense of individual lives often results in autobiography. Those accustomed to expressing themselves on paper may need little prompting. The intention is seldom that of being published. Usually the writer aims to leave a record for a younger family of what life was like for a vanished generation. But such authors are also writing for themselves. Driven by a strong impulse to gather, not only historical facts, but also important subjective themes from a lot of random memories, this can be an exploration of identity as it shows itself and develops through the years. Each person's story is not quite like any other, bearing the owner's unique stamp of self-hood.

Those to whom writing comes less easily may prefer to speak and perhaps record what they say on tape. But, without help, they can easily become stuck and lose heart. To save getting lost in a sea of detail, some sort of framework can be suggested, like chapters in a book. Some storytellers are best helped by being asked for their first memory, or for what they would judge to be the most meaningful episodes in their lives, high points, low points and turning points.

Life review as therapy was first advocated in America by the gerontologist, Robert Butler, 'as a normative, universal process triggered by a sense of approaching dissolution and death' (Butler, 1963: 65). By constant reminiscing, it is maintained that ageing individuals will keep a sense of self through all their bodily changes and feel less diminished as their faculties fail. 'Probably at no other time in life is there as potent a force towards self-awareness operating as in old age' (Ibid.: 302–3). A range of methods is suggested.

Memorabilia. Letters, diaries, scrapbooks and photographs of younger selves, if looked at after a lapse of time, may bring mixed feelings, especially when 'then' and 'now' pictures are compared. 'I still think of myself with dark hair' says an 80 year-old, 'but I'm now completely white.' She finds it hard to relate to a recent photograph. Nostalgia hurts less if shared with others, and groups of similar ages, who have experienced war and peace, together with personal losses, can give each other mutual comfort and understanding. A group in a residential setting may undertake to collect material for scrapbooks and displays, and derive a lot of benefit through working together. Such activities, you might say, belong more to occupational therapy than to counselling, but are nevertheless useful triggers for awakening good and bad memories or problems that still need to be resolved.

Reunions. 'An individual can look at himself in the context of other meaningful people and take a measure of where he stands in the life cycle' (Butler and Lewis, 1974: 167). At school or college anniversaries, contemporaries get together and are struck by continuity and change, both in the institutions and in themselves, which may bring shocks as well as surprises. Family reunions, such as golden weddings or 80th birthdays, with three or four generations present, will be celebratory but touched with a hint of sadness over what has been lost.

Pilgrimages. Visiting places where one has lived through a range of emotions is a powerful way of capturing the past. The picture retained in memory often proves inaccurate when compared with the actual place. Perhaps this is due to forgetting details, but often there is a real change in a landscape that has been covered in new buildings. One old lady decided that she would deliberately go back to a place where she had been conscious of perfect happiness, though doubting, even at the time, that she would ever be so happy again. The return to a still recognisable, though more prosperous, country made her neither happy nor sad, but at peace with herself.

Family Trees. Studying the ancestors helps establish one's place in history. 'One of the ways to resolve fear of death is to gain a sense of other family members having died before them' (Ibid.: 167).

These suggestions challenge client and counsellor alike, and provide guidelines for further exploration. Once the flood gates have been opened, we, as counsellors, need to tread carefully, so that the client does not get swamped by the power of the memories and emotions evoked. We may, before the session ends, feel we should nudge the client back to the present tense, perhaps with a smile or touch of the hand as a reminder of one's listening presence.

At its best:

> The success of life review depends on the struggle to resolve old issues of resentment, guilt, bitterness, mistrust, dependence and nihilism. All the really significant options remain available until the moment of death – love, hate, reconciliation, self-assertion and self-esteem. (Ibid.: 169)

The stories people tell are attempts to answer the questions 'who am I?' and 'why do I exist?' The therapist cannot give answers but may be able to help the client re-work the script and see the past as:

> a malleable, changing and re-synthesised series of previous life choices. History and identity are both made and discovered ... a good life story is one that shows considerable openness to change and tolerance for ambiguity. (Hyer and Sohnle, 2001: 51)

The following case material, without fitting neatly into a particular model, shows the importance in old age of being the author of one's own story, together with the eventual realisation that it can also be re-told by important others who had a share in the plot.

Rachael

In her mid 80s, this client found herself moved to a sheltered housing complex in the north of England, so as to be near the home of a niece, who she had never known well but who felt responsible for her. Rachael's only son lived with his wife and family in New Zealand and was prepared to delegate all decision-making to this cousin. Counselling had been suggested by the warden, who realised that her new tenant was lonely and disorientated and who also felt weighed down by a responsibility which she was reluctant to take on.

Rachael's first words to her counsellor were, 'I seem to have lost my life story'. The counsellor offered to help her find it. 'Do you mean you've forgotten?'

'Not exactly, but everything's so unreal. If this is where I belong, what's happened to the past? It's like a dream. Or is this the dream? It certainly doesn't feel like life.'

She had no friends, no familiar landmarks. The flat was too small for her furniture. The stove was electric whereas she was used to gas. The nearest supermarket was her least favourite, but there was no other choice. She was advised by the warden (and by her niece) to eat the lunch provided downstairs and meet the other residents. Then she could just get herself a snack for supper – no problem! Yet, for her, everything was a problem. She was surrounded by strangers. Her son sent e-mails through her niece. What she wanted was proper letters and photographs of her grandchildren. Her niece came fortnightly. She had a full-time job and a family to look after. Her visits were a duty. They talked about the weather or television programmes, nothing personal. Sometimes she brought flowers – from the same dismal supermarket – or chocolates, always peppermints, which Rachael had never liked.

The counsellor showed interest in hearing Rachael's story.

Rachael: There's so much of it – I don't know how to begin. I'm frightened of it slipping away from me.'

Counseller: You don't have to begin at the beginning.

Rachael: Well, I couldn't, could I? No one remembers being born. It's like death – we don't know that either.

Having established that her story had no beginning and no end, Rachael felt able to plunge into what she called 'midstream'. Without prompting, she realised that getting the facts right and their chronological order was not important. She wanted to remember her many friends and the exotic countries in which she had lived with an adventurous husband, who had made money and lost it again, a compulsive gambler, who had died in a motor accident without saying goodbye. But they had loved each other to the end – that was something to hang on to. Hanging on seemed to matter to her – could she write it down? 'I was a painter, not a writer.'

'Do you still paint?' She was diffident, like a child who had been told not to make a mess. There was no room to set up an easel. She might sketch a bit, but there was so little to look at, just houses – ugly modern houses. 'Could you paint your memories?'

'And my dreams?' She got interested in different mediums, opting at first for crayons and watercolours, moving to pastels – which did make a mess – and, for her most passionate memories, choosing acrylics, a new discovery. It seemed that her life was being given back to her – in a blaze of colour. But there was something missing – people. She was tired of living only for herself. Painfully, she realised that her son also had a story. With the counsellor's encouragement, she admitted that she had always put her husband first and that he had been a distant and irresponsible father. They had sent the boy to boarding school when he was just eight, assuming that a good English education must be what he needed, rather than traipsing from one far-off country to another, depending on her husband's latest whim. Their son never showed unhappiness, only silence. She said he never confided in her, nor did he ask for advice. As soon as he grew up, he got away, and now he lived at the other end of the world. He could hardly have gone further. In her old age, with no husband, she would like to have had her son near her, as a replacement. But he punished her, keeping himself and the grand-children away.

She saw her personal myth as that of 'The Prodigal Son.' Or was it 'The Prodigal Mother'? She asked herself this question without prompting from the counsellor. She resolved to write her son a long, honest letter. She also thought about how to achieve an easier relationship with her niece – and even with the strangers in the communal dining room.

She went on painting and eventually gave what she felt sure would be her last exhibition, in a gallery hired through a friend of the niece. The profits went to a children's charity.

It took time for Rachael to understand that her story could be more than an ego-trip, that the myths we live by can be changed and narcissistic wounds healed. Old as she now was, she could still take some responsibility for her life, and, though her day-to-day living arrangements might remain unchanged, she could continue to enlarge and enrich her inner world, by seeing the events of her past life as they had been experienced by people other than herself, and to do this without flinching from her own (and her husband's) distortions of the truth. By too much 'hanging on' to her own version of the story, she had obscured those possibilities for reconciliation that were still available to her before she died.

The good and mature personal myth is grounded in social and personal moral-ity. It is what you have created from the real resources you have been given. Mature identity does not transcend its resources; it is true to its context. The myth and the mythmaker must be credible if we are to live in a credible world. (McAdams, 1993: 273)

Ways of working with narrative

Despite attempts, ever since Freud, to give psychotherapy and counselling scientific validity, what in fact happens in therapy sessions is the telling of stories, and these stories being listened to in order to extract meaning from them, through being shared by the participants; this applies both to groups and one-to-one sessions. But there are numerous ways of attending to stories, just as there are numerous ways of telling them.

Psychodynamic practitioners use their clients' stories in order to detect unconscious processes underlying the problems presented, and these need to be recognised and worked through in the therapy. Personal stories are thus a means to an end rather than being of value in themselves. There is also, as the meta-story behind the personal, the myth (for Freudians) of Oedipus Rex, seen as having universal application regarding sexual rivalry and repression of murderous impulses. This powerful myth could be open to all sorts of different interpretations, but, for Freud, sexual repression was so fundamental to human experience, that he seems to have insisted on looking no further. Jung introduced a whole range of extra myths, classical, biblical and legendary, yielding many more interpretations for his dream-work and active imagination. Early psychoanalysts would have been steeped in ideas from a classical education, no longer familiar, even to those growing old today, many of whom come from cultures with different mythologies. It is worth noting that Rachael, the client described above, was conversant with the New Testament parable of The Prodigal Son, and able to use this myth and expect it to be understood, but such shared knowledge can no longer be taken for granted in today's largely post-Christian society.

McLeod (1998) points out that we 'inhabit a densely storied world', yet 'find ourselves acting as the passive recipients of waves of stories transmitted by television, newspapers and novels' (p. 68). We can still tell our personal stories – and therapy provides an acceptable outlet – but there is so much undigested material coming at us from all sides that it is harder to fit our individual stories into a cultural context. This situation can become bewildering and alienating, especially for an older generation.

A recent innovation within psychodynamic therapy is the theory of a core life-story originating early in life and repeating itself in a person's adult relationships. Luborsky and Crits-Christoph (1990) have developed the Core Conflicted Relationship Theme (CCRT) by which the therapist identifies, for instance, a wish (for love), reponse by the other (rejection) and response of the self (depression).

> The CCRT model is one of the strongest examples of how psychoanalytic practitioners and therapists have integrated narrative concepts into their approach, but without changing their basic model or theoretical assumptions. (McLeod, 1998: 57)

Looking at a series of seemingly different stories that clients bring to their sessions, the CCRT therapist detects an underlying pattern, the most usual being wishing for love and understanding, followed by a perceived rejection or being controlled by others, with subsequent disappointment and depression. If we apply CCRT to 83 year-old Rachael, her wish for love had been fulfilled by a husband who then disappointed her through his early death. Her son rejected her by moving to New Zealand and her niece controlled her. This for years had been Rachael's version of what had happened and her response was depression and withdrawal, until at last she managed to escape by changing her story. Her counsellor did not use CCRT, nor did she interpret Rachael's behaviour but encouraged her to find her own creative solution.

Changing the story

The most active methods to bring about change in clients' stories are probably those of the constructivist therapists (whose historic precurser was

Kelly (1955), the originator of 'Social Construct Psychology'). The aim is to work with ways in which people construct meanings through the different – sometimes conflicting – stories they tell. The client is invited to tell and re-tell the story of key events, and to do so objectively, subjectively and metaphorically (Goncalves, 1995). Therapy involves homework, for instance writing stories from different periods of life, and sessions of guided imagery to facilitate recall. Objectifying narrative involves re-telling in such a way that the listener is drawn into the story, by producing external artefacts (photographs, diaries, letters) and sensory cues to do with seeing, hearing and touching. Subjectifying aims to increase the story-teller's inner experience, for instance, 'How does the story make you feel now?' Great importance is given to metaphors and their origins in a person's life experience. The client is asked to construct alternative metaphors through images drawn from literature or art, and to use them, first in the sessions, and then in everyday life. Through these exercises, the client develops 'a continuous sense of actorship and authorship in his/her life' (p. 158). The overall aim is to facilitate change in how the client perceives and makes sense of the world.

Social Constructionist Narrative Therapy enlarges the perspective by seeing narrative as a bridge between individuals and the cultures into which they are born. A central aim is that of clients re-authoring their stories, having first deconstructed them from the dominant narratives of society, in so far as these may have impoverished the story-tellers' lives. Therapists adopt a 'not knowing' attitude towards their clients, thereby showing that it is the client, not the therapist, who is the expert on his/her story, and it is the client who is able to change it. Looking again at Rachael, a point came when even her renewed creative activity was not enough. She needed other people in her story and the recognition that they had stories of their own affected, and eventually changed, her version of events. The most important occasion on which Rachael found words for her narrative was in the long letter she wrote to her son, which was seen only by him. Her counsellor, a Rogerian enthusiast, saw her role as no more than facilitator, allowing the emergence of Rachael's hidden potential.

In what Erikson (1959) called our 'one and only life', we need eventually to accept the story we have been making for ourselves from childhood onwards, and look back on it with 'post narcissistic love'. In old-age, we reflect on what we have made, and perhaps, at the same time, distance ourselves from it, so that we can let it go, leaving only a memory of what we were for our descendants.

Jung, at 83, was persuaded to leave an autobiography. His concern was with narrative truth.

> I can only make direct statements, only 'tell stories.' Whether or not the stories are 'true' is not the problem. The only question is whether what I tell is my fable, my truth. (Jung, 1967: 17)

He ended the book with uncertainty about himself but a feeling of kinship with all things.

... that alienation which so long separated me from the world has become transferred into my own inner world and has revealed to me an unexpected unfamiliarity with myself. (p. 392)

We can, I think, infer that he was ready to let go of his life and that he was interested in the process of doing so.

Reflection and review

- Most of us have favourite myths or fairy stories. You may like to choose one of these to discuss with your colleagues and try to see why this particular story has special significance for you. What does it capture about your personal experience of life?
- Try to apply CCRT to some of the stories you find yourself telling about your life. Can you see a pattern emerging? Could this pattern be changed in any of the ways described in this chapter?
- Listening to some of the stories your clients tell, can you apply new metaphors to what you hear? In what way might that help to change a particular client's script?

6

Obstacles to Change: Avoidance, Resistance and Other Factors

Sometimes therapy becomes an obstacle race, in which it seems both sides are challenged and there are no winners. Counsellors, as well as clients, have their no-go areas which, despite having been through therapy themselves, they are still wanting to defend. Resistance has become a psychoanalytic jargon word to define, in Freud's mechanistic language, a force that obstructs access to unconscious thoughts and desires. There is also, both in an out of therapy, a conscious resistance, such as defending cherished and strongly held precepts. Carl Rogers does not mention the 'unconscious' but has much to say about awareness and being open to new experience, without preconceptions or fixed behaviours. The process of change, he insists, is fluid and must be allowed to flow. However different the metaphors, both Freudian and Rogerian languages are concerned with the blocking and distancing of free experience. As we saw in Chapter 5, it is often helpful to look for new metaphors to illuminate, and perhaps change, a person's outlook on life.

People are not of course obstructive just because they are old. As I hope I have already made clear, especially in Chapter 2, many of today's elders have proved themselves remarkably resilient in surviving and adapting to the revolutionary changes – social, political and attitudinal – of the 20th century. But it is not those who have successfully ridden the storm who are likely to become our clients. Those seeking therapy will be, as in any age group, people who have not managed easily to adapt to change, and one of the chief differences between them and our younger clients is that their defences have been set up and fixed for a longer period and may be clung to with greater obstinacy. This, in itself, may be an indication for long-term therapy.

Avoidance

Counsellors are usually trained not to regard a client's 'presenting problem' as central to whatever unease has brought that person into therapy. It is never easy to be intimate with strangers and it may take some time to win a client's trust. On the other hand, what is presented should not be disregarded, since it usually gives some hint of a more serious problem. Looking back to the case of Bob, described in Chapter 4, he presented himself as a flood victim, and had in fact lost his home, an event which was dramatic enough for an interview on national television. The trauma of the flood had left him disorientated, and his first few sessions were full of indecision about his future. But he soon showed signs of a more serious disorientation that had been with him since childhood and caused him agonies of doubt about who he was and where he belonged. He had got into the habit of avoiding certain words, for fear of them bringing on panic attacks. He was also full of shame about what he saw as his inadequacies, and it took time and considerable courage to face his fears and understand them.

Bob, who was in his 70s when he came to counselling, was born at least 20 years after Queen Victoria's death, so could hardly be described as a Victorian, but he belonged to a generation whose parental and authoritarian figures still held fast to what we tend to call 'Victorian values'. He would have been taught to keep his feelings to himself and never to show emotion in public. Sexual subjects were taboo, and sexual activity – especially masturbation – had to be kept secret. The blocks built up in youth had protected both his self-image and how he appeared to other people, but he was full of underlying fears. A younger counsellor needs to recognise the power of 'old-fashioned' taboos and how strongly maintained are the defences against admitting that the rules have been broken. In today's tolerant society, none of this should be dismissed as a fuss about nothing. However desperate a client's wish to move on and feel free, there may also be a backward pull to that earlier, more structured society, where certain things were simply 'not done'. These taboo feelings need to be respected even if deplored.

Obvious examples of avoidance are clients not turning up for sessions, arriving late or chatting about the weather or the news, instead of talking about themselves. Or bringing up crucial problems a few minutes before the session is due to end, with a total disregard of boundaries. There are also clients, so unable to face the end of therapy that they manage to avoid the final session, saying goodbye on the telephone and hiding tears by being able to ring off in their own time. These avoidances are not peculiar to old people but are often – it seems cunningly – manipulated, in the same way as children tend to persist, and get away with, controlling their parents and carers. Old people use forgetfulness, and it is often hard for the counsellor to distinguish intentionality from repression. In Chapter 4, I described an 87 year-old who 'forgot' to bring her diary to a carefully planned last meeting, and behaved as though she needed it to book further sessions after a summer break. On being challenged, she admitted to knowing it was the end but 'wriggling'.

Somatisation is a way of denying emotional problems, and it is particularly difficult for an older person's therapist to distinguish physical manifestations of these mental upsets from organic illnesses that need medical treatment. The old lady, who denied the finality of her last session, had initially been referred by her doctor for having a rash on her skin with no physical cause. The therapist ignored the rash and, when the client had vented her anger, it disappeared. Chronic Fatigue Syndrome (formerly called ME), is often diagnosed as depression but needs different treatment.

This is difficult to recognise in older clients, in whom a certain amount of fatigue may be expected. There seems to be a tendency in this age group to prefer physical illness to neurosis. Most older people have not been brought up to be psychologically minded.

Carl Rogers, describing the process of therapy, states that, in the early sessions, 'the individual has little or no recognition of the ebb and flow of the feeling-life within him' (Rogers, 1963: 133). The problems are external, with no sense of personal responsibility. Feelings are expressed but not owned. A person may say 'there were depressive symptoms' instead of 'I was depressed'. But, gradually, as trust in the counsellor increases, so does an ability to express feelings in the present. Intimacy, that at first seemed dangerous, can begin to be risked. The self ceases to be an object to be talked about, but becomes fully owned. Rogers echoes Sartre – 'The self is subjectively in the existential moment.' (p. 147)

For the Rogerian or 'person-centred' therapist, there is no fixed state in 'becoming a person'. People are always in process, that is always becoming, always changing. Our elderly clients may seem hopelessly stuck in the past or in distancing themselves from themselves, perhaps not at home in their ageing bodies. Or they may be so identified with bodily discomfort that they seem to lose the richness of an inner life that could continue to grow. The counsellor needs to meet each client as an individual, who can be just as open to new experience as those of us who are young or middle-aged. The optimistic approach of Rogerian therapy may be a help in reaching out to the person behind the body's pain.

Defence, resistance, repression

After looking at the ebb and flow of Rogerian language, how embattled these Freudian terms sound! Psychodynamic practitioners are trained to be more suspicious than their humanistic counterparts, in that they are always paying attention to what is not being said, to the distortions and disguises that clients adopt when trying to talk about their personal problems. Freudians never underestimate the power of unconscious forces, as if an underground movement was operating in secret against the law and order of conventional living. Freud, as early as 1895, was already wrestling with resistance as an impediment to analytic work:

> By means of my psychical work I had to overcome a psychical force in the patients which was opposed to the pathogenic ideas becoming conscious (being remembered) (Freud and Breuer, 1974: 352)

Resistance was seen to follow the analysis step by step. It was the analyst's job to point it out and discover what caused it. Through Freud's 'fundamental rule' of free association, present was linked with past and the traumas of early childhood revealed. In spite of a huge theoretical development over the past century, defence, resistance and repression (along with transference), have remained the bedrock of psychodynamic thinking.

The following vignette shows a strong resistance in an 80 year-old.

Millie

Millie was referred by her GP for being chronically depressed and lonely. He was not sure that counselling would help but suggested giving it a try.

Millie talked to the counsellor about her dog, Kim, who had died too young from terminal cancer. She had been persuaded to put him to sleep and felt like a murderer. 'It wasn't necessary. He wasn't in pain, just incontinent. They wouldn't do it to humans. I should never have let him be killed. I betrayed him.'

Counsellor: You speak as if he was human.
Millie: Don't go telling me 'he was only a dog'. He was everything to me – too young to die – it shouldn't have happened.
Counsellor: I'm wondering – was anyone else in your life too young to die?
Millie: Well, I suppose so, but it's Kim I'm mourning. Don't you understand?
Counsellor: I think I do. It's bound to be sad at first, when it's just happened.
Millie: Kim died two years ago, but it seems like yesterday.

The counsellor asked about other bereavements, but Millie insisted that there was no point in discussing them. 'Why dig up the past?' However, the story that emerged, bit by bit, was full of loss. First, there had been the death of her little brother when she was only six. She had been given a puppy to cheer her and that was her first dog, who lived to a great age and she was grown up and married before he died. After that, she called all her dogs 'Kim'. The counsellor wondered why, and thought perhaps it made for continuity in a changing world. 'Same colour, same breed, usually related', said Millie, though insisting that they were all individuals and 'part of the family – like having children.' It turned out that Millie had given birth only once, to a stillborn child. There had been three miscarriages. She told her story flatly, with no emotion. But when she talked about Kim – any of her Kims – she wept copiously. Her husband had died of cancer. 'Too young?'

'Perhaps – that is he didn't see 70. But he'd had a good life – and a lovely funeral.' The counsellor went on probing, but Millie turned on her angrily. 'Where's all this getting us? It's obvious you don't like dogs. You'll never understand how I feel.' Millie didn't come again.

This counsellor certainly seemed on the right track, but she got her timing wrong. With hindsight, she saw that she should have stayed with the dog and established a trusting relationship, based on here and now, before slowly exploring those other losses, and the profound pain that they would have produced if not displaced. By turning her back on the past, Millie had got on with an energetic life. At 80, she was having to let go of much of her activity as it was straining her heart. She would have liked another Kim, but would not have been able to give it the exercise a young dog needed, and she wouldn't accept an old one because it would die too soon. The future looked bleak and the past was affecting the present. She criticised those old people who lived in the past. Why dig it up? Perhaps the counsellor should have answered that question by suggesting that it was sometimes necessary to remember the losses and mourn the pain, in order to let go of what she was so afraid of facing.

> By demonstrating the reasons for defences, a person becomes more ready to lower them inch by inch as it becomes safer to face the feelings that they mask. (Jacobs, 1982: 94)

But one should never lose sight of the fact that defences are useful and, for some of us, some of the time, even essential. Indeed, if they work, why rock the boat? It is when feelings are vehemently denied, projected, displaced or split off that intervention may become advisable. Michael Jacobs advises going slowly:

> First accept there is a good reason for resistance; secondly, draw attention to the resistance itself; thirdly, suggest or attempt to discover why there is resistance; and finally create a sense of trust which enables the barriers to be lowered, in order to reach the particular feelings which initially gave rise to them. (Ibid.: 108)

Sound advice. But I would put the 'sense of trust' first, not last, in advising counsellors on how to set about their task.

Whose resistance?

The American psychoanalyst, Greenson, in a detailed study of technique, calls our attention to the 'what', the 'why' and the 'how' of resistance (Greenson, 1974: 107) with the intention of helping his readers to understand the client's (in his case, 'patient's') unconscious dynamics. But what about the counsellors' counter-resistance? Firstly, what is it that makes us uncomfortable in the presence of an elderly person? We usually want to help our clients to live life to the full with the same goals and hopes that we expect to have ourselves. It comes as a shock to realise that, for this person, future possibilities are diminishing and the ultimate goal will be that of facing death. What we resist looking at in our clients is likely to be what we have never dared think about. Secondly, why? Surely it must be because we still have unresolved relationships with parents and other senior figures, whose authority we thought we had outgrown, but whose influence again seems to threaten us, as we see it embodied in the here and now of the counselling room. Our determination not to look at the end of life begins to fall apart. The inevitability of death is not something we often think about, let alone put into words. So – thirdly, how do we cope with these uncertainties? Perhaps we try to reassure or abruptly change the subject. We may collude with the client's own denial, or perhaps we find ourselves focusing on those few safe issues that we feel adequate to address, without leaving the client much choice in the matter.

Patrick Casement, in his popular book *On Learning from the Patient*, writes both about resistance and control:

It is easy to rationalise that patients should not be allowed to control their own therapy, as if this might 'render the therapist impotent' – to use a familiar phrase. But if the therapist insists on controlling the entire therapy, might that not equally render the patient impotent? (Casement, 1985: 19)

When there is a stalemate, 'there may be something the therapist has not yet recognised or acknowledged, and *the therapist can be resistant too*.' (my italics) (p. 18)

Reluctance on the part of both counsellors and clients was highlighted in a survey carried out for Age Concern on counselling older people:

There is an inherent difficulty for some counsellors in dealing with older clients because of their own fears of ageing and their training may not have identified this as an issue. (Bennet and Cass, 1998: 5)

As for death:

There is a reluctance amongst young people – an embarrassment – to acknowledge that it is inevitable, and therefore the opportunities to talk are not made available. (p. 17)

Among counsellors, potential clients and the caring professions, quite serious resistance was discovered by the researchers, not the least from older people themselves to whom counselling is usually an unfamiliar concept. Older people often boast that they can 'stand on their own two feet'. One elderly widower, who had used a bereavement service and found it helpful, commented that he had friends in their 80s who needed help, but in general their attitude was suspicious. They would say, 'I don't want strangers in my house' and they had a fear of their names 'going down on a file'. This reluctance seems to be catching and service providers have tended to minimise older people's needs and to doubt their ability to use psychotherapeutic interventions.

Repression

'Why is it,' an old lady finds herself asking, 'that we don't get desperately upset by our various aches and pains, which we know will only get worse as the years go by?' It sounds a reasonable question, asked by a fully conscious individual as she faces bodily change and deterioration. One might say that her consciousness is of an unconscious process, which surprises her. And the answer must surely be, 'it's because of a merciful repression'!

One can think of many incidences of people unconsciously defending themselves from fear. When a deadly disease has been diagnosed and a person informed of its progress and prognosis, he will quite likely concentrate only on the minor dread of invasive or painful treatments, perhaps only realising if the immediate danger to life recedes that he might have died. If such a person should happen to be in therapy at the time, I find it hard to believe that his defences would not be respected, at least until such time as he is ready to face the sombre truth – carefully, and 'inch by inch'.

Ernest Becker, writing about death and its denial, insists that repression is not simply a negative force opposing life's energies, but lives on those energies and uses them creatively:

> Nature seems to have built into organisms an innate healthy-mindedness ... On the most elemental level, the organism works actively against its own fragility by seeking to expand and perpetuate itself in living experience; instead of shrinking, it moves towards more life ... it would seem that fear of death can be carefully ignored or actually absorbed in the life-expanding process. (Becker, 1973: 21)

The effect of trauma

Everyone experiences trauma of some kind, and an accumulation of crises and stresses that reactivate the worst that we have suffered. We cope in various ways depending on temperament, and many get by without outside help. But we need to remember that some of the present generation of old people have been exposed to terrifying events that included torture, and fear of torture, watching friends being killed and what seemed a complete reversal of the usual human values. And all this had to be endured with no hope for the future and no news from outside the hell of that experience. I refer not only to holocaust victims, but to the fate of hundreds of prisoners, wounded and tortured in the wars of the last century, and to the cruelty of dictatorial regimes, terrorist attacks and kidnappings that still go on. As counsellors, we need to listen carefully to a client's war stories to ascertain what level of help this person needs and whether we can supply it.

There are survivors who seem to be coping because they don't tell us what they feel. By not talking they may be hoping to forget. They have nightmares but keep them secret. They employ all the stratagems of avoidance and denial, consciously and unconsciously, in order to keep going, but find themselves trapped in a half-life with undercurrents of rage and terror. To quote one such victim:

> Not talking becomes a fixed habit, a way of shielding ourselves from those years, and this is doubly true for the victim of torture, who most certainly does not talk. I can write this now, but I have come a long way since the moment I first determined to confront my memories. (Lomax, 1996: 234)

It took him 40 years. Eventually, he approached the Medical Foundation for the Care of Victims of Torture: 'That meeting was like walking through a door into an unexplored world, a world of caring and special understanding' (p. 236).

The story of how he managed at last to meet and forgive the Japanese interrogator, who had been one of his tormentors, is told in his book, *The Railway Man*. Its last sentence is: 'Sometimes the hating has to stop' (p. 276). Meeting Eric Lomax, as an old man, I was struck by his serenity. Here, I thought, was living proof that what Freud called 'the talking cure' does actually work.

Trauma, if it can be successfully integrated with life experience, has been seen as an opportunity for psychological growth. Coping with major stress brings a sense of mastery and a possible base for questioning previous assumptions and developing wisdom in later life. 'We believe that the older person brings something better to the table of adjustment than those at other ages in this area (of trauma)' (Hyer and Sohnle, 2001).

Obstacles to counselling – failures in the system

Statistics show that out of seven million people with mental illness, 13 per cent are over 65, and that 17 per cent of suicides are in this age group (Thomson, 1993). But only a small minority of older people find themselves referred for counselling and, if helped at all to free themselves from isolation, may be offered 'tea and chat' and other get-togethers, often with people as depressed as themselves. We need to ask ourselves why we, as a society, are giving them such short shrift.

> Older folks do not 'want' psychotherapy. Problems can be represented in under use. It is best explained by the concatenation of reluctant elders to receive psychiatric care and a reluctant system to provide incentives for such treatment. (Hyer and Sohnle, 2001: 14)

Why, the authors ask, is there such collusion between older people and health care providers. They suggest that doctors do not recognise depression in old-age as a problem to be addressed by counselling, and this results in potential patients not recognising depression in themselves, or, if they do, refusing to admit to it as a problem. Hyer and Sohnle are describing the American scene and it seems not dissimilar to our own.

Research done for Age Concern in Britain (Bennet and Cass, 1998) shows many gaps in support programmes for older people, especially when it comes to setting up counselling services. Of the local groups who completed a 1998 questionnaire, 27 ran their own counselling services, 139 did not. There were differences of opinion on whether they should encourage setting up more of their own counselling services or act as gateways to other services in the locality. The way they saw their roles depended on what else was available. They might be looked to for financial support but it is not easy to attract funding in a climate of negativity among service providers and referral agencies, not to mention the older people themselves.

A variety of supportive roles for Age Concern groups were identified by the researchers. These were – advocacy, befriending, self-help support and peer health-monitoring. As gateways, they could undertake essential roles in giving information and advice, both by telephone and face-to-face, and thereby identify needs for emotional and psychological help. They could also offer information as to where to go for support. They needed close contact with other services in their neighbourhoods, to overcome their own (real or perceived) lack of credibility in the counselling world and any doubts they might have themselves about how counselling could help.

Older women

Depression and lack of self-esteem increase as women get older. Problems have to do with motherhood, the home, isolation and loneliness, death and dying, regret over childlessness, failure to take advantage of educational opportunities and often a regret over not experiencing the full range of their sexual potential (Jerome, 1994).

> She identified a surprisingly low rate of older women in counselling for parallel reasons. Firstly, older women's reluctance to accept the need for it and secondly, a tendency in providers of services to minimise the mental health needs of this group. (Bennet and Cass, 1998: 18)

Older people in residential accommodation

> A number of issues such as depression and alcohol abuse are going largely undetected, due to limitations of assessment and inherent ageism. (Bennet and Cass, 1998: 19)

Counsel and Care's publications clearly indicate that the emotional and spiritual needs of older people at home and in residential accommodation are not at present being met (Chester and Smith, 1997 and other publications).

Some groups of older people were interviewed and asked what they thought about counselling. Their reactions were, on the whole, negative. Most believed in 'getting on with it' and 'making the best of things'. Only one person knew anything about it, having been offered a bereavement visitor when her husband died. Most of them relied on their families and friends or went to the GP, who gave medication for depression. They also attended an over 60s club twice a week. Only one was interviewed individually. She admitted to extreme loneliness, and that, in between visits to the club, there was no contact with others in the group.

Age Concern's home-grown counselling courses are varied according to demand, who is available and qualified to take part in management, and the funds to pay professionals for managing, tutoring and supervision. Some, notably a well-established West Country scheme, run their own trainings. There seems an obvious need, whether part of an Age Concern portfolio of services or privately run, for closer contact between these organisations, more research and further dissemination of information to promote awareness. Only thus will resistance be overcome.

As we have seen, most counsellors in this field believe in an integrative approach, in which person-centred, cognitive behavioural and narrative therapies blend with the more classical analytical models. Here is a message of hope from a colleague who ran an Age Concern counselling group for many years:

> Spread the word through conferences and other events and publish accounts of the work. The good news is that very elderly people do benefit hugely from psychodynamic counselling and analytical psychotherapy. (personal communication from Laurence Roberts, Waltham Forest – Bereavement and Loss Support Services, 1993)

Reflection and review

- Two different counselling models have been shown in this chapter: humanistic and psychodynamic. Do you see them as mutually exclusive or do you think they can be combined, each perhaps enriching the other?
- Do you think Millie could have been helped by a counsellor with a different theoretical approach?
- What might make you aware of a client's resistance?
- What unresolved issues of your own might get in the way of being open with an elderly client?
- I suggest that, as a group exercise, you try to enter into the world of a torture victim and discuss your feelings with colleagues or fellow students. Try to be honest in facing whether or not you would be prepared to counsel a survivor. How might you help this client to break a silence maintained for many years?

7

Working with Difference

We have looked at ageism and the prejudices that tend to marginalise older people in our society as being unable to benefit from counselling because they are perceived to be 'past it'. We have looked too at what we, as counsellors, resist when faced with older clients and why, up till recently, so little provision has been made for them in terms of therapy, counselling or just listening. Difference, and how it is perceived, creates all sorts of 'isms' that we need to confront, notably 'racism', 'sexism' and what has come to be known as 'ablism'. If being old is, in itself, a disability, how much greater the disadvantage of being old and black, old and disabled or old and gay!

Multiculturalism

An important motivation for taking up counselling is a fascination with human nature in its varied forms. The stories our clients tell us may carry echoes of our own experience, or we may be shocked by traumas and struggles that we have never had to encounter. But, for those of us who trained in the UK a few decades ago in the psychodynamic, person-centred and/or cognitive behavioural models described in this book, the contexts of our clients' lives have been more or less recognisable as belonging to a familiar culture which most of us seemed to share.

We need to be clear about what we mean by the word 'culture', which, for our purpose, is probably best understood by those anthropolgists who have systematically studied the ways in which groups of people make sense of the world and their place in it. Haviland (1975) defines it as 'a set of shared assumptions where people can predict each other's actions in a given circumstance and react accordingly' (p. 6). Up till recently, many of us may have taken it for granted that our assumptions were shared by most of the people we were likely to meet, and that our reactions to what was said would be more or less accepted. Different cultures belonged far away in other continents and were unlikely to affect the way we lived and worked in the Western world.

The impact of immigrants and asylum-seekers has only gradually made itself felt. As the host country, we thought we had much to offer in the way of safety, tolerance, opportunity and all the benefits of democracy. But we expected those who settled in the UK to adapt to our way of doing things. Many of them did, and those born in this country have forged for themselves – with varying degrees of success – a multicultural identity. It is their grandparents who experience loss and loneliness in this transition. The problem (literally as well as figuratively) is not between black and white, but involves a number of ethnic groups, whose older members have been noticeably absent from psychotherapy and counselling services. Counsellors cannot all be anthropologists, but we can be open and imaginative. 'The core of multicultural counselling is a sensitivity to the possible ways in which different cultures function and interact, allied to a genuine curiosity about the cultural experience of other people' (McLeod, 1998: 163). As counsellors, we need to be modestly respectful of differences, and willing to learn from our clients that, for instance, a dualistic view of reality (mind versus body), which – whether we are fully aware of it or not – permeates Western tradition, is not necessarily the only view. Eastern holistic thinking, particularly in the field of healing, has begun to make some headway in the West, though it is by no means assimilated and still tends to be regarded suspiciously as 'alternative' and unscientific. We need to remember that many of our older ethnic clients have just as much difficulty in assimilating Western insights. Likewise, the Western concept of person-hood, as individual and autonomous, makes less sense in a collectivist culture, and Shakespeare's famous advice 'to thine own self be true' may not have much meaning for selves who are not perceived separately from the families and social groups that surround them. We must be prepared also for different attitudes to morality, with less emphasis on choice and responsibility and greater acceptance of 'karma', which determines a person's destiny.

With empathy and imagination, cultural barriers can be penetrated. On a simple level of shared humanity, we can recognise loneliness, loss, uprootedness and the strong generational differences that these older ethnic clients must be suffering. However different their world-view may be from ours, there will be much in their life-stories with which we can identify. A lot of research needs to be done on how to adapt our Western attitudes, especially as regards individual therapy. Meanwhile, the best we can do is to be flexible, and less strictly conventional, in the way we use it. We need to take nothing for granted and allow ourselves to question our clients with a genuine interest and desire to understand their differences, while, at the same time, being careful not to show the kind of curiosity that might rouse suspicions of being researched for the counsellor's own ends. A black pensioner had this to say:

> You don't need books girl. We are all different and all God's children. Don't go around putting us together like a basket of oranges now. I won't have it. (Alibhai-Brown, 1998: 81)

The black community

Black people have lived in the UK for centuries, so it is worth glancing at their history in order not to put them in one basket. Some were brought here as slaves. Others came to escape slavery. Many came from the West Indies to fight in the world wars of the twentieth century, for a king and country that they had been used to recognising as their own. In the second half of the same century, emigration was encouraged. As early as 1948, 492 Jamaicans were shipped to this country to help rebuild heavy industry and the new welfare state. By 1958, the community of Afro-Caribbeans had grown to 125,000. Most of them took unskilled, poorly paid jobs. These were people who arrived with great hopes. They saw themselves as having been invited to come 'home' to a country where they belonged on equality with white Britons. The reality was different. When they looked for lodgings, they encountered notices saying 'No blacks'. At work, they found themselves isolated. Everywhere they met with discrimination. These are the black people who have now grown old. If they ever come to counselling, white counsellors must be prepared for considerable bitterness and anger. Some of them dream of going back and ending their days where they had their roots, in a warmer place. But that would mean separation from children and grandchildren and even less financial support than they get by staying.

White counsellors must not assume that every black person comes from the Caribbean. Africans are fewer and arrived later. Often they came as students and never returned. Others were political refugees, their countries still in turmoil. Some, before they die, hope to return to 'all those ancestral spirits'. Like the Afro-Caribbeans, they have often been denied equal opportunities, even when they are qualified professionals.

There seem to be few services specifically adapted to black people's needs. Local authorities emphasise that service provision is 'open to all' regardless of race. If they make no use of existing services, one is told that 'blacks look after their own', or that there is not a sufficient number of them to justify separate provision. So older black people are invisible, their needs largely ignored. If day centres prove inaccessible or inappropriate, there is little hope that anything as specialised as a counselling service will be envisaged, nor can one be sure that the European or North American models of counselling would be what work best.

It is said that, in African culture, 'the individual is validated in terms of others' (Lee, 1999, p. 78). The emphasis is on family and collective survival. Many black people are practising Christians, who attend their own churches, where singing and shared prayers are common; everyone participates to the full, and the sense of community is stronger than in most white congregations. Pastors are often seen as traditional healers, as well as providing support for families in crisis. Black people are likely to consult senior family members and clergy before looking for professional help. But older black people are themselves the grandparent figures to whom the younger ones expect to turn, and they may find it impossible to reverse these roles. If they do eventually seek therapy, they may only feel at ease with black practitioners, but these are few and far between. However, if white counsellors get referrals – and they sometimes do – they should obviously accept the challenge and be prepared to adapt their usual counselling stance. It is unlikely that an analytic approach will have much effect. But black clients may turn out to be natural story-tellers and weavers of fantasy. Dreamwork may also be rewarding; Africans have a tradition of paying serious attention to their dreams. Anger will be important and a white counsellor may well be a target. Special anger-workshops can be set up, either with a mix of black and white or all black people. Both are worth trying.

Group counselling is likely to be these people's counselling option, focusing on links between personal/family problems and the political/ social world which they inhabit. Their sense of identity, being collective rather than individual, will be enhanced by working in a group that meets to explore, and take a pride in, what it means to be black. This can be seen as pioneering work, with few definite guidelines to follow. Only by letting ourselves be at the cutting edge of a new experience will we be able to bridge, rather than ignore, a painful, historical gap.

Asian communities

Although Asians form the largest ethnic community in the UK, the term covers a wide range of different races and religions and it would be unwise to lump them together as one group. They originally came to the UK because the British once inhabited, and also ruled, their countries. We cannot easily erase the effects of history, especially in white counsellors' dealings with older Asians, who still remember the British attitude of superiority in the days of the Raj. Yet many fought alongside the British in the second World War and deserve to have that recognised.

Indian independence, and its subsequent partition into India and Pakistan, caused horrific bloodshed and resulted in a wave of migration from the sub-continent in the 1950s. Some of these older immigrants have bitter memories. Twenty years later, Britain took in Asians expelled from Uganda by Idi Amin. Later still, a number of Vietnamese refugees found their way to Hong Kong, some of them coming on to Britain. Others came here to study, married British partners and stayed. Most Asians have settled in urban areas, both in London and northern cities. Many have been able to buy their own houses, though, with large families, there has been a lot of overcrowding. They are more likely to be unemployed than white people, though a fair number run their own businesses. Many of these people had unrealistic expectations about retaining their culture and religion intact. They were in for some shocks. A Muslim from Pakistan complained that his daughter had married a Hindu and no longer covered her hair. This mattered to him as much as if she had married a white Christian. He had almost lost touch with her. 'Our grandchildren are just totally English, no care for the elders, no manners. They laugh at us' (Alibhai-Brown, 1998: 87).

Some older Asians, particularly women and especially when employed in a family business, have not learnt to speak English. This, in itself, is likely to form a barrier between generations. At home, they may speak one of several languages – Hindi, Urdu, Gujarati and Bengali, to name but a few. Communication with grandchildren is apt to flounder, and that is often a source of anguish among people to whom the status of being a grandparent is an important feature of old age.

In the public sector, neither counselling nor psychotherapy are readily available. The stigma of mental illness produces shame, and talking about problems does not come easily. Depressed Asians often suffer in silence and resign themselves to fate.

SubCo

SubCo Elders Day Centre in Newham, North East London, is run by Asians to support the aged members of their community. This is a success story. Since opening in 1993, help has been forthcoming from Age Concern, the Social Services, the Housing Department and the Health Authority. Among other projects, the Shanti Counselling Service was set up in 1997 'for Asian elders wanting emotional support and wanting to share their experience in a safe place' (Annual report on SubCo Shanti Counselling Service, 1999). Four counsellors were originally employed to work in five different languages. Diversity of language has been a problem and sometimes the counselling has had to be done through an interpreter, a situation, which, however sensitively handled, must get in the way of communication between counsellor and client.

During 1998 (described as a honeymoon period), referrals came steadily from voluntary organisations, fewer from statutory colleagues and fewer still from Bengali organisations that had been contacted. Bengali elders were invited to a special meeting but, out of 50 invitations, only two groups responded. More successful were two SubCo conferences on mental health and counselling. Among the questions raised were 'What is mental health?', 'What is counselling?' and 'Is counselling appropriate for Asian elders?' There was found to be a lack of awareness about these Western concepts, due to the absence of appropriate information, but the Asians who attended participated fully and highlighted the issue of isolation, suffered by older people in their commmunity.

At one of these conferences, a counsellor, who had been working for two years with these clients, stated that they had been able to talk about their distress and engage at a deep therapeutic level. To quote from a grateful client:

> No matter how dull or unwell I feel, there is no way I want to miss these sessions. I eagerly wait for Wednesdays when I can come and talk to you because I just cannot talk about these things to anybody. There just is nobody around to understand me. (Ibid.)

Families and the roles that family members play are of great importance to such clients. Elders have traditionally been respected and are distressed when their Westernised children and grandchildren treat them casually and do not acknowledge their seniority. They look to the counsellor for authority and expertise, and this will be reflected in the transference relationship. Out of respect, the client may be unable to challenge the counsellor, but, instead, will act out disagreement by missing a session. We need to understand this reluctance, and also the client's family role. We need to focus on family issues but avoid any hint of taking sides. Traditional group therapy is seldom appropriate, though support groups may be helpful in overcoming isolation.

Aruna

The following vignette illustrates a cultural problem. The counsellor, in this case, was white.

Aruna had two names. For living in England, she called herself Anna, but, when at ease with people, she liked to go back to her given name. With her English counsellor, she introduced herself as Anna and only admitted to Aruna when she found herself able to relax and trust the counselling process. This took some time. She was painfully aware of cultural differences and knew England well enough to doubt whether family feuding and divorce would pose much of a problem to today's Westerners. She came from a high caste Hindu family and had escaped an arranged marriage by eloping with a man of inferior status, whom she thought she loved. Together they had made a life in England, but she was painfully aware of the rupture with her parents, who refused any further contact. She was soon disillusioned with her husband, who was continuously unfaithful and, having won his high-born prize, treated her thenceforth with the contempt he had for all women. Neither of them adapted easily to Western ways and, for years, she put up with his ill treatment. As she got older and lost both her looks and much of her vitality, he spent more and more time away from her, and finally asked for a divorce when he wanted to marry a much younger white woman. Aruna obeyed him, as she had always done, and the divorce went through, but she was bitterly ashamed of this final rift with her own culture. In the counselling sessions, she tried to hide her tears. For years, she had not allowed herself to cry, and now she found it hard to accept that she was being given permission to do so. 'How can you possibly understand?' she asked in every session, and would invariably begin her sentences with 'In my culture …'. She had been taught that her role in life was to be mother and grandmother, to give support to a new generation, not to give way to her own distress, but to accept her karma. It was as if she saw her sternly dignified mother watching her in disgust, and indeed she felt disgusted with herself for betraying her family values.

She had an only son, who sided with his father and clearly did not want her support. She resigned herself to a fate that would never change. Her counsellor encouraged her to think for herself, to make her own choices, to mourn the past but let it go. Aruna shook her head. 'In my culture …'. But she listened, and eventually took some positive steps to please herself. She joined the University of the Third Age and went to lectures. She attended painting classes. Gradually she picked up new friends, some Asian, some English, and could laugh when she fancied her parents' disapproval.

Her counsellor suggested that Aruna and Anna were coming together and producing a livelier, more tolerant person. Her son married a girl of mixed race, born in England, who wanted him to 'cut through the nonsense' and let her meet his mother, the grandmother of his future children. This meeting, and the giving back of what she had seen as her rightful role, was the beginning of Aruna/Anna's transformation. Her daughter-in-law moved easily between two cultures, and encouraged Aruna to adopt some English ways without losing her Indian traditions. She greeted her counsellor, dressed in a sari. It was clear that the time had come for Aruna to let go of Anna, without denying that she still had her usefulness sometimes. She could also let go of her counsellor. As for culture – perhaps that could be re-defined.

Aruna's daughter-in-law was a useful go-between in negotiating cultural differences. She could do this from the inside, due to her own mixed inheritance. The white counsellor was useful in a different way. She was an outsider, wanting to learn from her client a respect for the Hindu tradition, while, at the same time, giving her a taste of what it was like to be English and part of a more open society. Comfortable as it might have been for Aruna to remain, as though in a ghetto, with an Indian counsellor, she also needed the feeling of being welcomed into the country and culture that she now inhabited.

Bearing in mind that our Western emphasis on autonomy and self-actualisation has less relevance to Eastern notions of identity than participation in the family or group, we should be open to our clients' indigenous healing backgrounds. Questions that need exploring are how far we, as therapists, can equate ourselves with the traditional shamans, whose treatment embraces an undivided mind and body, as well as a strong spiritual dimension that is not separated from the material world. Unaccustomed as we are to prescribing herbal remedies or acupuncture, we are at least beginning to accept them as part of a recognised holistic approach, even though using them may not be part of our own repertoire. Family and group therapy may take on something of a traditional ceremony, in which respected elders and past family members, even though dead, still have parts to play. A likely aim is the promotion of interpersonal harmony.

These are generalisations. What we need is an openness to our clients' otherness and a strong wish that they and we should learn from each other our different modes of being human. We will be meeting individuals in various stages of adapting themselves to living in an alien culture. An important part of our job will be to facilitate this process.

Old and disabled

Ablism is a new word but not a new 'ism'. There will, of course, be counselling issues with young disabled that do not apply to the old. With the latter, we are inclined to expect disability as concomitant with being old, even if the lack, whether of sight, hearing or movement, has been present since youth. Or we may regard old age as, in itself, a disability. As in racism or sexism – along with ageism – this is another example of prejudice and stereotyping of individuals. Doctors do it because their concern is with the illness, not the individual, so Mrs Smith becomes 'the coronary in Intensive Care', thus acknowledging only one aspect of the many-sided human being who is currently receiving treatment. Medical training may encourage turning individuals into cases in order to focus on what medicine can do for them, and also, perhaps, to desensitise those who have to cope on a daily basis with people who suffer and die. Even so, we appreciate those doctors who also find time to recognise, and have conversations with, the person – Mrs Smith – whose heart is in trouble.

As counsellors, we need to take a holistic view, and it is important not to catch prevailing attitudes of other carers – whether of neglect or intrusion – that tend to dehumanise old people in need of help. We need empathy and restraint; empathy to experience in ourselves the client's powerlessness, and restraint in offering our help at the right time and in the right place. Before taking an old person's arm in anticipation of a fall, it is tactful to ask first if the help is wanted, even though it is often hard to stand and watch determined assertions of independence without intruding our effective younger selves. Too much effusiveness can annoy as much as too little. An able-bodied lady in her late 90s was irritated rather than flattered when she was described as 'wonderful' for her age. The implication was that people were surprised to find she actually had two eyes, two legs and behaved normally. She was prepared to take risks rather than having to be preserved as a showpiece in a metaphorical glass case. She would say, 'I've got to die some day. Meanwhile, let me live the way I choose.' The only reason for interfering would be if her activity were to put other people's lives at risk. Her daughter was thankful that her mother had never learnt to drive a car, and that she would never have the job of trying to stop her! When and how to let go of such pursuits can sometimes be a major counselling issue.

Deafness is one of the most frequent disabilities and, being more invisible to onlookers than blindness, help is often less forthcoming. Young people get impatient when asked to speak more slowly or repeat themselves. They feel 'told off', blamed for the other person's disability, which is often denied. 'Why can't Mum stop telling me I mumble, and get herself a hearing aid?' Deaf people get paranoid as they watch inaudible conversations and imagine themselves being talked about behind their backs.

Loss of memory, if severe, can be worse for all concerned than deafness. I will write about Alzheimer's in a later chapter. The disease has been so much publicised that those of us who forget names and where we put things often get nervous, wondering if the first symptoms are beginning to appear. We may compare notes with friends and laugh with each other, but only up to a point. An 80 year-old asked her therapist if she had noticed her memory getting worse. She wanted an honest answer and was relieved when this loss was recognised and accepted. In such a case, the only reassurance that a counsellor can give is that the total loss we call dementia will not necessarily result. It could happen to any of us but, to most of us, it will not. Meanwhile, all we have to cope with are partial lapses. The missing word often comes back later, especially if we can manage not to worry about it.

Respecting, and expecting our elders to function unless or until they admit to needing help, should be our natural reaction to ablism. What we need is patience and empathy, both of which often seem to be lacking in institutions, especially when carers are overworked, underpaid and largely untrained. The result is a general attitude of infantilising the residents, sheltering them from stimulus and challenge and laying on what have been called 'pretend' activities to pass the time.

> The sanitised description of the absence of real experience may be 'care', but in fact this arrangement may be more for the benefit of others, who prefer to deny the real emotions and aspirations of older people. (Stirling, 1996: 407)

The very real losses of old age tend to be underestimated, especially by younger carers, who avoid looking at their own futures. The positive attributes of ageing are also real, but not easily experienced in an ambience of negativity.

Old and gay

Any counsellor seeing an old gay man or an old lesbian has to remember how hidden and shameful their orientations used to be in the time of their youth, when 'coming out' was unthinkable. Unlike the ethnic or disabled minorities, their way of life was invisible. The modern phenomenon of coming out has been described as a 'developmental process' (Zera, 1992), in which case the older gay person will have missed an important rite of passage. Enforced secrecy may have added an edge of excitement to sexual activity, but it also induced guilt and a fear of being found out. The oldest among them grew up at a time when male homosexuality, even between consenting adults, was a punishable offence. Internalised guilt and suspicion may have persisted into old age, together with the 'survivor guilt' of having outlived so many who have died of AIDS. Counselling HIV and AIDS sufferers is specialised and unlikely to come the way of more generalised counselling services, but it will doubtless have affected at least the margins of most people's lives.

They may call themselves 'queers' or 'old queens' but with an uneasy bitterness, those being the terms used by homophobes before the advent of 'political correctness'. They will certainly challenge the tolerance shown to them by 'straight' counsellors of either sex, and will be constantly on the look-out for a heterosexual bias, and shock or disgust regarding their preferred sexual practices. The counsellor may experience involvement with what seems an alien culture, just as much as would be the case if the client were to have a different-coloured skin. Similarly, he or she may become the target for all the homophobic hate and abuse suffered by the client in a less tolerant age and only partially withdrawn in today's more accepting climate. We need to be aware of a heightened sensitivity to the language we use in counselling sessions, to show genuine interest but with no hint of censure, and, most important of all, to affirm the normality of the client's life-style and relationships. We are not there to 'cure' the 'disease' of homosexuality but to validate the individual gay person.

The following case material shows the aridity that can result from conforming to traditionally accepted moral standards.

Robin

Robin was approaching 70, the retirement age for clergy, when he asked for counselling. He had a shock of white hair, which had once been blond and curly. In his lined face, it was still possible to see traces of the beautiful boy he had once been. 'I'm a wreck,' he said, 'or worse than a wreck — so dried up inside that I just walk around like a zombie. I can't look at the future without dread — there's nothing to live for.' 'But you're asking for help,' said the counsellor, 'that must mean you have some hope.'

'My spiritual director told me to come, but I don't know what good it can do. It's too late to start leading a different life.' The counsellor suggested that it was never too late and that retirement opened doors to all sorts of new opportunities. Then she asked what sort of 'different life' he had in mind. 'I've always been a good boy,' said Robin ruefully. 'I've loved people, but I haven't actually sinned.'

'Sinned?' Robin had been much loved. He was an only child in whom his mother delighted. When his father had gone away mysteriously, he slept in his mother's bed. He would like to have stayed there but Father soon came back to claim his rightful place. Very much later he heard that Father had been sent to prison, and it was later still that he discovered what the sentence was for. 'Sodomy,' said a boy at school, 'disgusting!' Robin consulted a dictionary and then the book of Genesis, but made no connection between this punishable sin and the attention being paid to him by the choirmaster, who would stroke his curls and kiss him on the lips — as if he were a girl. He was confused and embarrassed and relieved when his voice broke and he left the choir for more manly activities. In adolescence he fell in love, but not with a girl. Then he understood and was frightened. He began to fall behind at school and an understanding chaplain guessed his trouble and reassured him that it was only a phase; he would grow out of it. So, all his life, Robin waited to grow out of sex.

From school, he went to theological college, which was followed by military service. Thus he entered an entirely male world, which he never wanted to leave. There were many loves. He was agonisingly tempted and full of shame, but he never broke the rules. When he started work at his first parish, he was increasingly haunted by feelings of difference. His sermons were too intellectual. Despite his time in the army, he was, according to his vicar, out of touch with the congregation's feelings. He was told that his vocation was to teach. Later, as a university lecturer, he felt at home, as though the institution was his family. All vacations were spent with his mother. He and his father avoided each other. He fell in love with his students, but they moved on and he had to let them go. He was intimate with them, even romantic, but there was no sexual activity.

In middle-age, he began to feel he had lost his way. If he expected promotion, he would have to publish a book. When he lectured, he used other people's words. Now he looked inside himself and found he had nothing original to say. People's expectations made him panic. He read everything he could find about homosexuality and learned that his orientation was thought by some to be genetic. So – like father, like son. It was a curse from which there was no escape. He became afraid of putting any ideas of his own on paper, as though, by writing from the heart, he would reveal his true nature. There was never anyone in whom he could confide.

The crisis came when his mother died. She had been the only person to give him unconditional love – but would she have done so, he wondered, had she known his secret. He took her funeral but broke down afterwards and cried for weeks. He was given anti-depressants and offered psychotherapy, but preferred to keep his guilty secret to himself.

In his 60s, he had to retire from his university work. He was given a light-duty parish and a minor diocesan job. He felt lonely as well as more and more embittered when he realised just how many gay clergy, without officially coming out, had secured some of the top diocesan posts. He avoided their friendship but raged inwardly that he, who had not sinned, should be so unfairly punished. 'Punished by who?' asked his counsellor. She then put it to him that no one had punished him except himself, and that he had internalised all the homophobia, both real and imagined, that he had experienced throughout his life. She wondered whether the way forward in his retirement might be to make friends with like-minded gay people, without being ashamed to be with them, and to throw off the guilty secret that had so spoiled his image of himself; in fact, even at this late stage, perhaps he could come out and be proud of it. He might, she suggested, find that he could help younger clergy wrestling with the same problem. 'But these days,' he said angrily, 'There's no shame. Far from wrestling with the problem, they revel in it!' He then added more thoughtfully that there was still homophobia around, and he knew, for instance that bishops were required never knowingly to ordain a gay person.

He felt relaxed with his counsellor. He told her that, in spite of her hopes for him, he was dubious about the future, but grateful for her positive acceptance of him, whether gay or straight, as a whole person. No one had done this for him before. He had never allowed it.

As counsellors, we need to look hard at our own feelings of alienation when faced with differences, and question any latent homophobia we may be carrying with us. We should also be confident enough in ourselves to be able to refuse the challenge if we feel so uncomfortable with a client that our prejudice is likely to hamper the therapy. We need empathy, but we also need honesty.

Ageing lesbians, unlike thair male counterparts, were not engaged in anything considered illegal, but they experienced social rejection and parental disapproval to a much greater extent than those who are young today. This resulted in isolation and loneliness, in that a vital aspect of their identities had to be driven underground, condemning them to the half-life of ageing spinsters in an era when marriage and childbirth gave women status and respectability. The death of a partner had to be mourned in silence. Even today, such bereavement is not officially accepted and the only comfort may have to come from the gay community. But the older lesbian has not often 'come out' and perhaps feels, just as Robin did, that it is too late to turn her life around. An obvious loss is that of the children she never had, the opportunity having been missed in mid-life, allowing no time for second thoughts. Although lesbian couples can now use donor sperm to become pregnant, that would have been unthinkable in the days before these older women reached the menopause. Creativity can sometimes be channelled into artistic pursuits, but if this dries up, or was never strong, old-age may indeed be empty, leaving doubts as to life's purpose. Gay men mourn their looks. Lesbians may feel they have missed out on home-making and companionship. What can a counsellor do in these circumstances?

We should never underestimate the importance of listening and being there, especially when a previously hidden life-story is at last being revealed. But, in affirming their normality, we must refrain from regarding these old gay people as special, that is, different from any other ageing group. Many old people, without being gay, are lonely, bereaved, and/or childless, and no amount of counselling is going to give them back what they have lost or never had. Living fully depends on a person's inner resources, and all that any counsellor can do is to help a person to discover the mainspring that motivates his or her life.

'Classism'

There is one more 'ism' that seems worth mentioning, though we hear less about it than formerly, and have coined no adequate word to describe it. Although we like to think that class distinctions are fast disappearing, our older clients may still have fixed ideas about their place in society. A woman who had spent her whole working life 'in service', came to counselling when she inherited enough money from her employers to enjoy a comfortable old age. According to the standards of their time, these employers had been kind and caring and showed their appreciation by a generous legacy. This former servant, emerging at last from her downstairs status into a world of equal opportunity, found herself furiously angry at what she had missed. She needed to work through the pain and loss that she would never have dared to explore till now.

What I choose to refer to as 'classism' also works the other way round and is sometimes called 'inverted snobbery', which shows itself in criticism and mockery of accents and customs belonging to a dwindling minority, who were accustomed to servants and still struggle to pay for privileges such as private medicine and private education. Though many have adjusted to today's do-it-yourself world, others feel helpless and are overcome with nostalgia for the old certainties of class and status. They may feel alienated from children and grandchildren, who have grown up in a more flexible society. Or they may feel guilty, as though having to take the blame for the inequalities of a previous age. Such people should not be dismissed as snobs. They are not pretending to occupy a position that was not given to them by society, and they are as much the victims of social change as used to be the case with the servants whom they once employed. It goes without saying that, should they become our clients, they need our respect, not for rank and social status, but as ageing and no longer privileged human beings.

Reflection and review

- I suggest making a list of any prejudices that you feel able to admit to. Can you share these honestly with either one person or a group?
- Think about how you might adapt your counselling technique to make yourself more available to a group of elderly black people and how you would do this. Then do the same exercise with a group of elderly Asian people. What differences do you see between the two groups?
- What disadvantages and/or advantages do you see in cross-cultural counselling? Think about how you might feel if you were a white client and your counsellor was Asian or black.
- Do you think gay people should be counselled by gay counsellors, or are there some advantages in the counsellor coming from outside the gay community?
- Can you honestly say you have never recognised homophobia in yourself?

8

Relationships and Withdrawal

The next three chapters will accentuate the experience of loss in old age and its multiple manifestations, not all of them obvious to those of us who are younger.

When parents and partners die, patterns of relationship die with them. But families go on and the elders have to make a generational shift. They may find themselves respected, or their advice may be ignored. 'The past' wrote the novelist, L.P. Hartley, 'is another country. They do things differently there' (Hartley, 1953). It is hard to be dismissed as irrelevant and to be seen as having nothing worth offering to a new generation, a prospect that is particularly bleak for those elders who experienced rejection earlier in their lives, and who, without knowing it, have bequeathed their insecurity to sons and daughters.

A secure base

Bowlby (1980) describes attachment behaviour as seeking to maintain strong affectional bonds. The need for a secure base begins in childhood and is vitally necessary for survival. Children who feel unsafe and threatened with abandonment by those they love, experience extremes of anxiety that may persist into adult life and seriously affect their capacity to relate to others, whereas security in childhood, and a feeling of being loved and valued, makes people feel good enough about themselves to love without clinging, to respond easily to strangers and to make new friends, even late in life. Studies of people's attachment patterns (Main and Goldwyn, 1995; Fonagy, 1996; Holmes, 2000) show the influence of parental handling and have been classified as secure, avoidant, ambivalent or disorganised, according to whether parents have been responsive, rejecting, inconsistent or influenced by trauma in their own lives.

Attachment theory is akin to object relations in its insistence on a self in relationship rather then the classical Freudian preoccupation with libido development in an infancy driven by conflicting instinctual drives. Bowlby considered that the need for attachment was 'intrinsic to human nature, not some childish propensity to be outgrown with maturity' (Holmes, 2000: 163). I am suggesting here that this quite normal need continues into old age and that the degree to which an old person can adjust to loss and changing circumstances depends on early childhood attachments.

Jean

Jean was referred for therapy by a church worker on account of her depression, apathy and seeming inability to help herself. Jean insisted that her depression was just as 'terminal' as cancer or AIDS and she was angry that nobody was willing to help her, either by giving her hospice care or gently bringing her life to an end. She had written to the Euthanasia Society without receiving the response she hoped for. Left to herself, she would not take the responsibility of committing suicide, but was prepared for a doctor to do it for her. Her life, she said, was useless and nobody cared.

'You seem very angry', said her counsellor, and Jean showed surprise. She seemed unaware both of how she felt and the impact of her feelings on others.

Her counsellor was not the only person to whom Jean was turning for help. She was currently having acupuncture, homoeopathy and anti-depressants. She also talked to her vicar, who promised to pray for her. 'But God doesn't answer.'

She had no friends, only acquaintances and those who regarded her as a 'duty'. One of these had telephoned and apologised for not calling before. 'Why bother?' said Jean and banged down the receiver. 'But you wanted her to bother,' said the counsellor. 'No I didn't. What's the use?'

There was silence. The counsellor could not think of any reply that would not turn into an argument. Or – worse still – some sort of false assurance that she, at least, did care, and everything was going to be all right. But Jean was uneasy in the silence. She sighed, moved about in her chair, brushed a hair off her coat. She even tried a nervous laugh. Then – 'You can't help me.' The counsellor murmured that she was trying, to which Jean retorted, 'That's what they all say.'

Sometimes she played Bridge but her concentration was going. At 78, she could no longer play golf. 'I can't just sit still all day.' She went through a catalogue of other people's suggestions. She did not knit or sew; she had never liked reading; television was 'tosh'. She lacked the energy to invite people for meals. 'Nobody cares. Why should they?'

'But you want them to.' Yes, she admitted that she wanted someone to do things for her. She couldn't cope any longer with paying bills, getting the roof repaired … She had lost her temper with the neighbour's child, who kept throwing a ball into her garden and coming round to fetch it. Now she had antagonised the neighbours. 'But they're not my sort of people.'

'Then you don't want to try and put things right.'

'Of course I don't.' Another silence. 'I'm wondering,' said the counsellor hesitantly, 'who exactly are your sort of people.'

'Oh – you know. Or – if you don't, I really can't explain.'

Her voice, most of the time, was harsh and angry, but now and then there was a plaintive note. 'We never kept Christmas. Mother wasn't up to it.' No one in the family showed feelings. There were no endearments, no treats. Father left when she was in her teens. As the only girl, she was expected to stay at home and look after her mother, who never thanked her for it, only complained if Jean failed to do what she wanted. Her brothers fought in the war and one of them was killed. This was said without emotion. When it was her turn to be called up, she welcomed the chance to get away. She became an officer in the ATS, responsible for a platoon of girls. 'I did it well,' she said. 'I could be quite bossy. But that doesn't mean I liked it.' After the war, she did social work with no proper training but with people of her 'own sort'. It had been a mistake to move away from London and expect to make new friends. One brother was still alive but too disabled to visit her. 'Even if he did, he would expect a meal, and I hate cooking.' She was not prepared to make the half-hour journey to where he lived. 'Anyway,' she said, 'what's the point? He's just as depressed as I am. It must be in the genes.'

The counsellor felt she was being dragged into her client's claustrophobic world. It was as though every time she tried to open a door, it was shut in her face. All that Jean wanted was to be looked after and no one was doing it. She would really like to live in a residential home, where everything would be done for her and no decisions would have to be made, but first she had to sell her house. She put it on the market but complained that no one came to see it.

After 30 sessions, Jean decided that counselling was no help. She left abruptly.

Jean's attachment style could be called 'avoidant'. What she had never had, she longed for, but could not show her longing. As a young adult, she had given an impression of self-suffiency but admitted that it had felt unreal, and, sure enough, it collapsed when she lived alone and found she had no inner resources to sustain her, no routine to follow or person she had to nurture. Jean had clearly started life without a secure base, and this affected her ever more strongly as she grew old. Her counsellor never succeeded in breaking through her general helplessness, or inspiring hope in what seemed to Jean an uncaring world.

'Avoidant' people cannot express what they feel. Those who are 'ambivalent' lack a safe container for their feelings. Parents have not been rejecting but inconsistent in their support, leaving their children with little concept of relatedness. In old age, such people may cling to anyone who gives them their attention and they have a great fear of abandonment. The more disorganised these people's parenting has been, the more they look for, and fail to find, a secure base from which to live their lives. The counselling room, hospital, or old people's home may, to varying extents, fulfil some of that need.

Bowlby and his followers respected Freudian analysis but their work had a different emphasis. Instead of theorising about childhood trauma with no hard evidence except that of different types of neurosis encountered in adults, the attachment theorists concentrated on the child's disturbance when separated from the mother, and how much separation could be tolerated, especially at a pre-verbal level when a few minutes may seem like for ever, and the infant has no concept of the mother's return. Tests on children were backed by experiments on young monkeys, who were found to show the same separation-anxiety as infant humans, thus giving an ethological as well as psychological basis for attachment theory. Not only did both species show fear in the presence of perceived danger, but also in the absence of all that they could recognise as safety. As we have seen, too much absence can damage future relationships. With the losses and separations of old age, it should be no surprise if the earlier anxieties revive, especially when the body weakens and the environment changes.

Jean's therapy may have broken down through lack of warmth on the counsellor's part. She was not able to provide the secure base that her client so desperately needed. She was not able to forget herself and be 'there', like a secure mother for her child. Silence, which can often be fruitful, was tantamount to rejection. The counsellor's own insecurity probably reinforced Jean's anxiety. It seems that what they both avoided was intimacy.

Attachment and disengagement

Old age is, on the whole, easier for those who can mourn their losses but also let them go. Cummings and Henry (1961) introduced 'Disengagement Theory' to explain older people's withdrawal from their social milieu as a natural process. Instead of relationship, there might be a turning inward, finding time for reminiscing and making sense of their life-stories. The danger of such a theory is that it could be seen as a justification for neglecting ageing relatives and having low expectations of their needs. If this becomes the cultural norm, old people could too easily detach themselves and play the game according to 'the dominant social rules' (Scrutton, 1998: 122). They do not want to make demands or to be seen as complaining.

Parents and grandparents usually want to invest a lot (though not all) of their energy in future generations. The continuation of family may eventually make it easier to die. Before death, there may be a withdrawal of quite so much attachment to one's own routines and an acceptance of change, as not neccessarily for the worse just because things are different. 'To go with the flow' is a useful admonition, suddenly much in use, and all of us, including the old, might be happier if we could respond to it.

It seems to me that attachment and disengagement are not either/or choices. Healthy individuals, throughout their lives, may swing between these extremes, and we should be careful in our assumptions. It is important for would-be counsellors neither to jolly their clients into sociability, nor to suppose that withdrawal is always pathological. Loneliness is seldom alleviated by being pushed into getting together with a crowd of ill-assorted people or being given meaningless activities just to pass the time, as though time is a nuisance to be got through, instead of something precious to enjoy without hurrying. Old people in residential homes may feel they are back at school and bullied into developing a team spirit, with never a moment to sit alone and think. They know that being alone is not the same as loneliness and that one can be lonely in a crowd. Winnicott wrote a famous paper on 'The Capacity to be Alone' (1958), in which he describes the child as first learning to be alone in the presence of its mother, whose love is gradually internalised and permeates the person's future solitude. Storr challenges the view, held by most of today's caring professions, that 'intimate personal relationships are the chief source of human happiness' (1989: 5). He believes that the capacity to be alone is also necessary if the brain is to function at its best and that 'learning, thinking and maintaining contact with one's inner world are all facilitated by solitude' (p. 28). As counsellors, we must be careful not to intrude when our clients are silent except in cases of obvious need for mothering and containment. We must be sensitive to an old person's body language and facial expression. Does that far-away look mean lostness or tranquility? Are those gestures restless or enjoyably lively? If we were looking after a baby, most of us would respond instinctively. With the old, we need to recognise that there may be some regression to an infantile state, and react as we would to babies, without fuss or clumsiness.

Families

One of the problems of the way most of us live today is the decline of the extended family, which had always had a place for its respected older members. Traditional ties have been broken. The young want independence and mobility. Their careers may take them miles from their original homes. In counselling isolated older people, one often comes across instances of daughters moving their ageing parents to a granny flat or sheltered housing near to where they have moved themselves, often with the best intentions, only to create more isolation for the old person, now surrounded by strangers in an unknown environment, as well as having only minimal contact with the much-too-busy younger generation, who initiated the move.

The old need to adapt to changing patterns in family life. They are no longer in charge. It is hard for them to take a back seat and watch middle-aged offspring making what seem like grave mistakes and wrong decisions, rather than fulfilling expectations of what one wants them to be.

A mother's love for her children, even her inability to let them be, is because she is under a painful law that the life passed through her must be brought to fruition ... It is not easy to give closeness and freedom, safety plus danger. (Scott-Maxwell, 1968: 8)

Not only does she have to let them be but to accept their adulthood and recognise that roles are now reversed. The younger generation has the power to decide how and where their parents are to end their days. Often they also hold the purse strings. A counsellor can help parents to stand up to their sons and daughters, to think things over clearly and specify their own choices, but also to admit defeat or even come to trust that their children's solutions may, in the circumstances, be the wisest. If the generations can maintain a continuing respect for each other, these all-important decisions may be made without undue pain, and solutions worked out that save family members from being a burden to each other. Family therapy, if available, can sometimes put problems in context and perhaps bring about acceptance and reconciliation between the parties concerned. But that is beyond the scope of this book.

In my experience, a daughter whose mother was in therapy asked if she might have similar help for herself. She was referred to another agency. There were hints afterwards that mother and daughter were relating more smoothly, but therapeutic help for each of them was kept separate, with the usual barriers of confidentiality. Curiosity on the part of the mother's therapist would not have been appropriate.

Ruth

Ruth was an 80 year-old mother who found it extremely difficult to let go of her son, Paul. He had married in his early 20s and Ruth had been particularly fond of his young wife, Emma, seeing her as a replacement for the daughter she had never had. But the marriage had ended in bitterness, and this was her reason for seeking help. Paul was hurt and angry that his mother seemed to be taking Emma's side, and he did everything he could to prevent them getting together. Ruth had nothing good to say about Paul's second wife. 'How can I just drop the mother of my grandchildren, who has been such a good daughter to me?' She now looked at her son through Emma's eyes and began to find fault with him. But she also blamed herself for having allowed him to be evacuated to America during the war. 'I thought only of his safety' she kept saying, even though no one had ever blamed her, least of all Paul, who had been quite happy without her. 'When he came home, we were strangers.' With Paul's marriage and the challenge of a new family, Ruth's mothering skills had at first been appreciated. When Emma was young and inexperienced, Ruth was always on hand to help with housekeeping and baby-minding. But inevitably, as the children grew up, Emma gained confidence and Paul, resisting parental pressure, developed ideas of his own. Ruth felt dismissed. As she grew older, and especially after her husband died, she began complaining that her family never informed her about what was going on, her opinions were not asked for and no respect given to her age and experience. They may have criticised her; she certainly criticised them. She had to get older still, frail and nearly blind, in order to realise just how much her second daughter-in-law did care for her and the trouble she took about her welfare. By the time she finished counselling, she seemed to have forgotten her former criticisms and declared herself lucky that Paul had such a thoughtful wife. All her life, she had looked after people, needing to be needed. It was her way of being in control and it was hard to be the recipient of other people's care. Letting go was the main theme of the therapy.

Must sex be taboo?

In a survey some years ago, 100 people over 65 were asked what they felt about growing old. Only one admitted to missing sex – 'Dare I mention it?' How does this reflect the attitude of our society and the expectations, or rather non-expectations, the young have of the old?

If the old are sexually active or have erotic fantasies, the young would rather not know. Despite the permissive society, there seems to be one taboo that persists – sex is only for the young. For those who were children before and during the second World War, the subject was shrouded in secrecy. There was no sex education at school and parents, if persuaded to talk about it at all, tended to be vague and embarrassed. Schoolchildren speculated among themselves and were sometimes able to share snippets of information – 'If you'll promise to be my best friend for the rest of the term, I'll tell you a secret.' The secret was menstruation. Then there was masturbation, which was probably practised extensively by both sexes but caused shame and the threat of madness. There was an assumption that girls should be virgins when they married – though boys were generally expected to have had some sexual experience – and sometimes these girls turned out to be ignorant virgins, with only the vaguest notions of what was in store for them. Those girls who did step over the boundaries, did so in extreme secrecy and had somehow to discover for themselves some means of contraception. Getting pregnant was much dreaded and sometimes resulted in back-street abortions which were often damaging to health.

For these children, who have now grown old, life seems to have come full circle, and again the door is closed. 'What is this new disease called AIDS?' asked a 90 year-old of her daughter. The answer was as elusive as the one that she herself had given many years before when her daughter wanted to know about intercourse and the birth of babies. Yesterday's unenlightened children tend to be treated as though they have forgotten or never known the secret.

It seems that, in every generation, sons and daughters prefer not to think of their parents as sexual beings. This may have something to do with fear of incest, but is also culturally determined. The media presents us with countless variations of sexual behaviour, but lovers on stage and screen are usually young. Sex between the elderly, if shown at all, is likely to be treated as a joke. The advent of Viagra caused a stir, with a few brave couples discussing on television the difference it might make, or had made already, to their sex lives. The taboo is only grudgingly lifting. Most people are embarrassed and would rather not know.

The fact of being old does not in itself determine how much libido is retained. It often has more to do with health problems, particularly cardio-vascular disease, diabetes, prostate trouble or the side-effects of drugs, which are sometimes over-prescribed. There are also social factors such as having no partner, or collusion with the intolerance I have just described. Women worry about the menopause, assumed by some to be a 'deficiency disease', and, to them, the end of their sexual attractiveness. Men have a fear of impotence. This often leads them to boasting about their virility, and perhaps boosting it by turning to a younger woman instead of the post-menopausal wife. Couples often find themselves out of step with each other and it is not always the husband who is the more sexually demanding of the two. As I have described in an earlier book:

> When a woman of 65 told her therapist, somewhat wistfully, that she wanted to 'sing in her vagina', she was painfully aware of what could no longer be ful-filled. Her husband, meanwhile, was quietly mourning his own loss of potency. Both felt isolated, too proud, and also too shy to communicate their feelings to each other and thereby make possible a new kind of intimacy, less linked with giving each other orgasms. (Butler and Orbach, 1993: 31)

In such a case, a counsellor might agree to work with both together, act-ing as a catalyst to improve communication, so as to explore what they could still give each other, with less emphasis on performance and more on intimacy. To quote Betty Friedan:

> Woman or man, what we all need is some new way to touch, know, love each other the way we really are now, which is not for any of us the same as when we were twenty, thirty, forty. Surely there is something else to be known and felt and said about love in age – yes, love that gets beyond the insoluble dilemmas of the male/female imbalance, the youth obsession, the pressures and terrors of penetration, impotence, the measure of Kinsey and Masters and Johnson, the rages and jealousies that tortured our youthful and middle-aged sex. The fan-tasies and dreams of youth cannot sustain us or satisfy us in age. Maybe new possibilities of intimacy have to evolve beyond the ways of our youth – inside or outside the old forms of marriage, friendship, family, community – if they are to nourish us in age. (Friedan, 1993: 215)

A difficulty in counselling older people, who have been strictly brought up, is their view of sex as immoral or indecent, and the self-blame attached to still wanting it, leading sometimes to denial of their human need for bodily contact, all of which may result in depression. Masturbation is pleasurable, harmless and a relief from tension, but only if practised with-out the shame, which was instilled in childhood, and which is likely to persist into old-age. It is also a lonely occupation. The longing to touch and be touched may be met (though only in part) by hugging grandchildren or handling pets.

  Counselling can help break down barriers of reticence, shame and self-blame, but opening up the subject is never easy. Counsellors need to face the prejudices of society and, more important still, their own feelings of discomfort in recognising old people as sexual. We need to tread carefully, always remembering the heavy taboos that surrounded the topic in the earlier lives of these clients. We may meet women who never talked about it, even to their husbands, and men who would not dream of having such discussions with members of the opposite sex. Female counsellors (especially if fairly young and attractive) may arouse sexual feelings in their male clients, who will want to touch them and perhaps expose themselves. It is obviously important, in these cases, not to show shock or distaste but to point out the inappropriateness of such behaviour in the counselling setting. If the old man persists, he may have to be warned that the counselling will have to stop, or perhaps he could see a male counsellor. Young counsellors should be careful of the language they use. Medical terms for body parts, words such as 'penis' and 'vagina' may not have featured in an old person's vocabulary. It is worth listening to the client's private language, which will probably sound less coldly clinical and more personal.

In allowing the old to be sexual, we should also bear in mind that some have moved beyond sex and changed their focus. They may, like Socrates, be able to declare: 'To my great delight I have escaped from it and feel I have escaped a frantic and savage master' (Plato, 1908: 3). A post-sexual stage of relief and tranquility is certainly a possibility, but if it does not come about naturally, cannot be forced to happen. A lot depends on whether an old person's life is still full of new interests or only full of regret for what has been lost. A counsellor may be able to stimulate those interests or encourage frank discussion of the regrets. Most important, as always, is sensitive listening without shock or distaste.

Reflection and review

- Think about how you would react if an elderly client fell silent. How do you think you could distinguish between feelings of unease and feelings of serenity?
- Do you think the theory of needing a secure base would help in understanding some of your older clients? How do you think separation-anxiety might affect the counsellor/client relationship?
- Imagine yourself talking about sex with an elderly client, and what words you might use. Are there particular features that you might find difficult or embarrassing?
- How would you cope with counselling an old man who made sexual advances to you? Do you think you could remain calm and keep your professional stance?

9

Loss: Retirement, Bereavement and Diminishment

The most obvious loss is that of friends and loved ones through death, a loss that is made public by traditional ceremonies of burial and mourning, which, though less formalised than they used to be, still act as 'rites of passage' for both the mourners and those mourned. But there are other losses, less publicly recognised, and counsellors need to be aware of their importance.

Retirement

The only ceremony that, sometimes though not always, marks a person's retirement from work is a staff leaving party and the presentation of some suitable gift, accompanied by a short speech of thanks for work done, and a goodbye toast. After that, the retired person goes home, sometimes to an empty house, and gets on with what is left of life. The prospect of moving the official retirement age from 60 or 65 to 70, because life expectancy is longer these days, is provoking considerable discussion in the workforce and also in the media.

> Of course there is no ideal age for retirement and never can be, since some of us are born longing for retirement almost as soon as we put our shoulders to the wheel and others cannot face the prospect of idleness until they have both feet in the grave; nor does age always bring with it wisdom and experience any more than youth guarantees energy and enterprise. (Worsthorne, 2000)

With so many workers facing redundancy, or early retirement in their 50s, there is a trend in some leading companies to keep, or hire, older staff and introduce flexible pension schemes. The BBC is said to be employing post-retirement staff on contracts and some banks have brought back older managers because of their skills and experience. Sometimes 'it's good to be grey'.

But there are other workers counting the years or days before that longed-for date when they can throw off tedious routines of wage-earning and grab their pensions. It depends, of course, on job satisfaction. Though there are many for whom only the work-place is life-enhancing, there are also plenty of clock-watchers, yearning to fulfil their dreams or put their feet up. Greater flexibility is, of course, the answer but, as counsellors, we may find ourselves faced with people who, whatever their expectations, are finding it hard to manage without a given pattern for each day and the companionship of colleagues, for whom they find themselves mourning almost as though they had died. Faced with the empty years ahead, they may look on retirement as a waiting room for death. There is a dangerous threshold to be crossed, which is seldom recognised as such, and, for some, it may prove altogether too traumatic. If unprepared, they may actually die, often of heart disease.

Robert

Robert was caught by the Civil Service rule of retirement at 60, a rule which, up to that time, had not always been rigidly enforced. It was a shock to realise that, instead of fulfilling what had seemed quite a realistic ambition for future promotion, he had achieved all that he would ever be allowed to achieve in what turned out to be his last posting. He had always been too busy to think about ageing but now felt he was being labelled by others as 'past his prime' and only fit to be 'put out to grass'. At 59, he had been at the height of his powers. At 60, he became ill with an accumulation of minor complaints that sapped his energy. 'So they were right,' he concluded. 'I'm past it.' It took time to build another life, though he did eventually manage to throw off his depressed mood and embark on a quite different second career, finding himself suprisingly at home in the world of business and finance, which had formerly been alien to him.

Robert was a person who today might have been helped by some preparation. Pre-retirement courses are now on offer in many of the private as well as public sectors, and it is advisable that any counsellor, likely to be treating someone about to retire, takes the trouble to find out what is available locally. To give an example: my county council targets teaching staff for two preliminary sessions, when still in their 40s. The focus is on practicalities and covers personal financial planning, making a will, pensions, investment and tax advice. This leads to Part Two, between the ages of 55 and 65, depending on the proposed date of retirement, and is more thorough, covering two days and giving an update on superannuation and pension, as well as sessions on home security, health, diet, leisure, travel, making the most of one's time, coping with bereavement and attitudes to retirement.

There are similar courses for the council's public-sector staff, with three days of sessions that include pension entitlement, health and leisure, security, personal safety and financial information.

There is also a three-day WEA course, whose emphasis is on practical matters, with a whole day spent on finance. There is a so-called 'Death Day' about bereavement, funeral arrangements, insurance and bequests. About 30 per cent of those attending have been found not to have made wills; half never discussed retirement with their spouses. Sometimes couples have come on the course together. On the last day, there is a discussion on relationships and the effect of retirement on married couples. When retirement courses first came into being, all the issues were practical. Only gradually did psychological problems emerge. Research revealed that two years before retiring, people worried about money. Two years after, they were more concerned with the meaning of life.

It is not, of course, the counsellor's task to give practical information other than pointing a client in the right direction. Public libraries supply details of available courses.

Ian

This is a case, unfortunately typical, of an advertising executive who was suddenly made redundant in his mid 50s after a venture employing him overseas came unstuck. Back in England, Ian applied for several suitable jobs but was turned down each time for being too old in a young competitive world. He had never had the confidence to found or run a company of his own – though this was what his ex-colleagues suggested – but preferred the position of being second-in-command to a boss whom he trusted. He came reluctantly to counselling on the suggestion of his wife. 'I'm all right really,' he said, 'but the family expect me to be up and doing, not to vegetate – that sort of thing.'

'What would they describe as vegetating?' asked the counsellor.

'Oh – you know, going to the pub, walking the dog, reading who-dunnits. But they're right, I suppose. The holiday mood is wearing off.' The counsellor was determined not to hurry him. His family and friends kept giving advice and he seemed unable to respond.

'I tell my wife to stop worrying. I'm waiting for the right thing to turn up. She's impatient, thinks I'm really pathetic. She's probably right.' The counsellor pointed out his repetition of how other people were 'probably right' but that he was not prepared to take their advice. 'You want to choose for yourself.'

'Do I?' He looked surprised. 'I'd rather someone actually wanted me, and I just had to say yes.'

The counsellor tried to explore his lack of initiative, as coming from early in his life, with a stepmother who never valued him, preferring her own children from a previous marriage. He admitted that a 'can of worms' might be opened up, but he wasn't asking for psychoanalysis 'at his age'. The counsellor was struck by this case of internalised ageism, but Ian felt this was her 'hobby horse', not his, and apologised for not being a more interesting client.

Things did turn up. He produced a beautifully illustrated brochure for his parish church. 'How did you know I was in advertising?' he asked the Rector.

'I didn't,' was the reply. 'I just thought you might be the person I was looking for.' Many months later, someone else showed signs of wanting him and he found employment locally with a small agency, where he was happy to work for a much younger boss. This lasted well past the usual retirement age, after which he felt he had earned the right to 'vegetate' and be helpful round the house when he felt like it. The counsellor was frustrated at not being able to do more than recognise his 'bereavement' at finding himself so suddenly out of a job, and accept his need not to be hurried into deciding what to do with his life.

Our society tends to equate what we are with what we do, and most especially, with a profession by which we earn money. Those no longer earning may feel their identities have gone missing. Being a pensioner, no longer contributing in an obvious way either to the economy or the community, seems to turn us into second-class citizens. This is an exaggeration of the Protestant work ethic and of internalised ageism. We may also be dreading the loneliness of empty hours, of all our days being so exactly alike that we lose our way in the calendar. Life no longer has a recognisable shape. Many of us feel driven to fill the space with voluntary 'good works' and thus hope to assuage (unrealistic) feelings of guilt. Working in charity shops, sitting on political or church committees and ferrying the old and disabled to hospital appointments are all jobs that need to be done by someone, but, before plunging in, I suggest that it is worth asking oneself: 'Does that person have to be me? Is it what I am best suited for?'

Retirement is an important transition, a time for self-questioning. At last one is able to explore a range of new interests. There is still a chance, before old-old age saps all energy, to learn a new language, take up painting or sculpture, travel round the world, get in touch with long-lost friends or find more modest ways to enjoy new opportunities. A lot, of course, depends on one's financial position, but, for some people, freedom may be just as important as money.

Therapists and counsellors, especially those in private practice and self-employed, may choose to continue working long after the usual retirement age. In working with an older age group, maturity is probably an advantage. For a time, we may cut down our work-load to just a few suitable clients, while continuing as supervisors or tutors. But eventually full retirement will have to be faced. One of my colleagues wrote to me:

I suppose people vary in the extent to which their identity is tied up in their work. I'm sure however that I can't be too unusual in discovering that the whole business of being a therapist was central to my being ... the balance of my psychic equilibrium was upset when I gave up that role.

These feelings are not peculiar to therapists. I am sure that many teachers, doctors and clergy feel the same, though they may describe it differently.

Worthwhile jobs, like happy marriages, need to be mourned before we can let them go.

Retirement has no history. In our society, there used to be leisured classes, workers and paupers. Paupers were sent to asylums and workers to workhouses, where they laboured till they dropped. There was nothing much in the way of state relief for any who risked staying in their own homes, and it would not have occurred to older workers to retire at any specified age. There was only the inadequate Poor Law and no state pensions until early in the 20th century. Pensions were given to wage-earners as rewards for their services, not as entitlement to relief in old age. The concept of retirement is still alien to much of the developing world, where families work in the fields or in their homes and help each other, the older members doing lighter tasks as they weaken. But all this is slowly changing as Western standards upset the old certainties.

Now, in the computer age, we are all living through a period of change, as machinery becomes different and there is lighter work that older people can easily manage. We are living longer and, even more important in this context, staying healthier, so that there is a willing and capable workforce, made up of people whose children have grown up and left home, whose parents have died, and who now have time on their hands. Patterns of employment are also going through rapid change, and, with longer working lives, people are increasingly moving through more than one career. Others are self-employed and can make their own retirement decisions. A great deal can be achieved at home with a computer. What all of us want is choice.

Freud's prescription for mental health was to love and to work. Winnicott, a generation later, stressed the importance of play. 'It is in playing, and perhaps only in playing (that) the child or adult is free to be creative' (Winnicott, 1971: 62). Ian's family described him as 'vegetating', implying that there was something shameful about not working or looking for work. For Ian, his job had been work and play. He had enjoyed it. His title had been 'Creative Director'. He gladly let go of directing but would like to have gone on being creative. He was not enticed by any of the retirement jobs suggested to him, such as doing accounts for a small firm or chairing the Residents' Association in his neighbourhood. He wanted to play.

Those whose jobs have not been fulfilling may welcome the freedom of being retired. I knew someone who, living alone in her 70s, with her books, painting materials and stereo equipment, exclaimed that she felt herself becoming a child again, but a child with the freedom to do whatever she liked, without having to put away her toys at bedtime. The very old and the very young may find themselves on the same wavelength. Children often find they play more with their grandparents than with their parents, who are always busy working.

After years of compliance in a monotonous but demanding workplace, some of the retired may find they have lost their capacity for play. Perhaps something we can do for them as counsellors is to help them remember their childhood play, pick it up where they left off and develop it creatively. But for those who continue to mourn the loss of gainful employment, loss of status in the community and the satisfaction that their work was in some way of use to the world, a counsellor can sometimes help by showing them that there are still, nearly always, some choices they are able to make. Retirement shuts familiar doors but may well open new ones. It is a question of knowing where to look.

Bereavement

The death of important attachment figures is, for many individuals, the worst trauma they will ever have to face. It may be easier for the young and middle-aged to recover from bereavement, even though, one could argue, they are less prepared for its impact. On the other hand, the older people get, the fewer opportunities lie ahead for new relationships, achievements and adventures. It is of course impossible to generalise, but I think we should assume that the effect of bereavement on older people does not lessen, even though they have already suffered previous losses and separations. If they have coped before, they will probably cope again, but each new bereavement brings a new grief, and, even after long illness, culminating in coma, the onset of death is shocking in its finality.

For many of us, regardless of age, the death of a partner, with whom we felt ourselves to be 'one flesh', is the most wounding experience of a lifetime. The only loss that is equally distressing is the death of one of our children (whether in infancy or adulthood). A mother will describe such a death as 'all wrong' and say 'it should have happened to me'. In these cases, the bereaved person looks on the world as turned upside down. I don't think one gets over one of these major bereavements. At best, one gets used to it and gets on with life. The Queen Mother, who was a widow for 50 years, is reported to have said to a bereaved friend, 'No, it doesn't get better, but you get better at it'.

Much has been written about mourning and the stages that bereaved persons are seen to go through, as identified by Elizabeth Kübler-Ross (1970) and others. I confess to some scepticism over any packaging of experience into recognisable stages, though I can see that it may be some help to carers and also to counsellors, but only with the proviso that each bereavement is unique and that we should be prepared for a more chaotic process than it is possible to categorise. What is expected to happen can turn into what ought to happen, and well-intentioned carers may be too intent on looking for 'stages' to recognise what is actually happening in a bereaved person's psyche. I also believe that we should be wary of measuring, in months or years, the time it takes to recover from a loved person's death, or of deciding at what point excessive grief should be called pathological. Despite this warning, I think it is worth looking at these stages in the context of bereavement counselling.

Michael

There are six stages that I would like to explore in connection with this client, a 75 year-old widower, who was referred by his GP three months after his wife's death. Although he did not at first talk easily, he was able to communicate that his loss of a 'perfect wife' was hitting him harder now than it did at first. 'It was so unbelievable,' he said. 'I floated through the funeral in a sort of daze. Someone told me I was brave, but I wasn't because I hadn't any feelings. Friends paid me a lot of attention at first, and then there were things to do — reading and answering letters, giving away her clothes. Now there's nothing. People don't want to be with me any more, not when I'm like this.'

'Like this? You mean numb?' His counsellor had been told that *numbness* was how people felt in the first stage of mourning, *numbness*, then *denial*. She had not listened to Michael carefully enough to pick up that the loss was hitting him harder now than it did at first. 'No good crying,' he said, 'over spilt milk. She's gone and I've got to look after myself — shopping, cooking, that sort of thing.' He blew his nose.

'A good cry might help — even over spilt milk.'

'Eh? Oh that. Just a turn of phrase, doesn't mean anything really.'

'I took it to mean,' she persisted, 'that you're not allowing yourself to mourn.'

'Well, it won't bring her back.' There was silence. He fidgeted and she thought she should say something, but he was the first to speak. 'You're too young. How can you possibly understand?' More silence. What could she say? A tear ran down his cheek. 'Damn you,' he said, why d'you have to hurt me more?' She thought — he wants to *distance* himself. How can I get him to accept his loss and begin to mourn? 'You're too proud', she said, 'to show me what you're feeling.' There was no answer. He turned away and they stumbled through the rest of the session.

Her supervisor suggested that he might want to tell her about his wife and also describe her death, reminding her that the newly bereaved need, above all else, to talk and be listened to. He had already told her that no one wanted to be with him while he mourned, and now this applied to herself. If she showed no empathy (meaning being really with him) no wonder he couldn't open up.

Michael went on coming. He cried openly and was *angry* — with the doctors for not keeping her alive and with himself for being 'such a big baby'. He had so absorbed other people's ageist attitudes that he used them against himself. 'Even my daughter says I should pull myself together.' The counsellor discovered that this daughter was the same age as herself. Too young to understand? 'But I'm not saying that, am I?'

'No, but you probably think it.'

'Do I?' She smiled at him and for the first time he smiled back. Then he thanked her for sticking with him.

Like the daughter, she often longed to escape from his negativity. She found herself contemplating her parents' inevitable deaths, even her own, and needed considerable support to be able to go on seeing him. They worked together for a year of endless repetition, feelings of guilt, blame, self-neglect and physical illness. Decisions were made only to be revoked. Often he seemed to reach a turning point, but plunged again into despair. He looked very frail and the supervisor advised the counsellor to keep in touch with his GP.

The anger kept coming back and he blamed everyone for his loss – doctors, nurses, the counsellor for having no magic panacea – everyone except his wife, who was *idealised*. Never, never could anyone match her. 'Sometimes I *search* for her in other people – I even think I see her in the street. Then I think I'm going mad. There will never be anyone half as good.' He began to cry.

It was hard to break through his eulogies, but eventually the counsellor managed to say, 'You talk as though she was a saint. Didn't you ever have rows, or misunderstand each other?' 'Sometimes,' he admitted, 'and that makes it worse. I keep blaming myself.' More boldly, she found herself saying, 'You daren't let go of this perfect image. Only when you manage to say something about her weaknesses, only then will I come anywhere near knowing what she was like.' Then she added softly, 'And I'd like to know. Really I would.' He was shocked into silence. It was an uncomfortable session.

Michael never admitted that what the counsellor had said made a difference, but, soon afterwards, there was a change. He made the difficult decision to give up the home he had shared with his wife and moved into a sheltered housing complex in the same village. He made some new friends and found himself helping old people who were weaker than himself. He was surprised at having his efforts appreciated. Eventually he could let go of his counsellor, but not without genuine mourning and the ability to say how much he would miss her.

Michael's counselling covered at least five of the six stages his counsellor had been led to expect, but as she became more skilled, she stopped feeling she had to tick them off in order – numbness, distancing, denial, searching, anger and finally acceptance. It had been like learning to drive a car and gradually being able to go through the gears without being conscious of each move.

Rogers (1984) believed that clients find their own solutions. The counsellor helps by encouraging them to feel the full extent of their grief and to realise that it is acceptable to express it. Those who have difficulty with words may be able to paint or sculpt their pain. Unconditional positive regard, maintained at all times, ensures mutual respect. The client does not need the counsellor's advice or reassurance. What is important is that the counsellor attempts to enter the client's world, however alien it may seem, without fear or pity, but with an acknowledgement that the suffering is being accepted as real and can be imaginatively shared, regardless of the listener's youth, gender or other difference.

Feeling and expressing the pain is not, of course, enough in itself, but a basis for moving on to consider options for the future. Michael had to become more realistic about what and who he had lost, before finding the strength in himself to create a new way of living and to make new friends. The counsellor had been an 'enabler', not a magician.

We have already looked at reminiscence and the value of telling stories. In bereavement, it sometimes helps to create a story for the person who has died and also to place that person in the past and say goodbye. The gestalt empty chair can also be a useful aid in that the client gets the feeling of having a conversation with the loved person, perhaps to resolve past conflicts or just to say 'I love you' one last time.

How people face bereavement invariably has roots in the past and this is one of the reasons why counselling, especially in the psychodynamic mode, follows the same course in these cases as in confronting any of life's major crises. We need to remind ourselves of Erikson's emphasis on basic trust in infancy (1959), of Bowlby's attachment theory (1980) and Winnicott's 'good enough mothering' (1941, 1971) to understand whether, in old age, individuals can stand up to life's set-backs with resiliance and fortitude, or whether, with no one to lean on, they fall into despair. In so far as extreme old age brings second childhood, not in the sense of serenity but of dependence, it may be full of fear and mistrust, or there may be a renewed spirit of adventure. One recognises the child in the old person.

Susan

Susan, who was now 77, had never married. How could she leave her mother as her father had done soon after her birth? She was the only child. She stayed with cousins once a year. Sometimes they took her to France or even Italy, where she enjoyed the sun and visiting art galleries. She got on well with their children until they grew up and got bored with her. While she was away, she wrote to her mother every day. During her childhood and adolescence, there had been several different 'uncles' staying, or even living, in the house. They would often play with her, sometimes rather boisterously. One used to sit her on his knee and tickle her. At first, she found this fun, especially when he told her she was a pretty little girl, but some of his games frightened and hurt her. She didn't want to upset her mother by complaining, but was relieved when the uncle went away and was, in due course, replaced by another, who ignored her. In her teens, she avoided men, worked hard at school and liked to feel she was helping with the war effort, even though distantly, by knitting socks for sailors and keeping chickens to augment the rations. She enjoyed eating their eggs but cried when the chickens were killed for Sunday lunch. Her mother teased her for what she called her hypersensitivity.

It was hard to say when their caring roles got reversed. It was a gradual process. There were no more uncles and Mother was often ill and depressed. As time went on, Susan found herself in a position of power, filling her days with the responsibilities of housekeeping, cooking and attending to her mother's every need. Mother made dramatic statements about wanting to die, but Susan learnt to take no notice. The doctor reassured her that there was nothing to worry about and that her mother was remarkably strong and would probably live to a great age. Neighbours felt sorry for Susan and told her she was overworked and needed a rest. So did the cousins, who went on offering holidays but no practical help. Susan shrugged off these other people's worries. 'What else would I be doing with my life?'

Mother lived to see her hundredth birthday, revelling in the importance of the occasion and her message from the Queen. Susan made a cake and lit 100 candles. She asked the neighbours and the vicar for tea and dressed Mother in her Sunday best. The old lady beamed at everyone, Susan included. 'What would I do without my devoted daughter?' Some of those present wondered what Susan would do without her mother. At last she would have freedom, but would she know how to use it?

A few weeks later, Mother died peacefully in her sleep. To Susan, she had seemed immortal and her death was a shock. She coped with funeral arrangements, correspondence and sorting out possessions. People congratulated her on her efficiency. The cousins gave her another holiday. After that, she faded from sight. It was assumed that she was getting on with her life. Susan came back to the empty house feeling immensely tired. Then she sat down and cried. It was the vicar who first got worried about her. He found her withdrawn from people's company, slovenly in appearance and neglectful of the house. It was he who suggested counselling. She agreed because she was used to being told what to do.

There was no difficulty in getting Susan to express feelings. Her eyes were always red with crying and each session was full of tears. The counsellor felt as though she was with a small child, who had lost a pet or favourite toy. She wore her mother's clothes without altering them to fit. On one occasion, she came with odd shoes, one black, one blue. The laces were undone. The counsellor found herself stooping to tie them. Susan's regresssion was such that she seemed to be crying out to be looked after. It was hard to believe that here was a 77 year-old who, for years had run a household and been her mother's sole carer.

The counsellor wondered if she had the experience and know-how to take this client on. Should Susan perhaps be referred to a psychotherapist or analyst, who was accustomed to coping with bizarre cases. But already a strong transference was emerging and she felt the weight and incongruence of mothering a woman 35 years older than herself. That was the role being imposed on her. The supervisor reminded her that the transference relationship was never more than symbolic. She also discussed the different kinds of mothering that could be experienced. Close as Susan had been to her mother, could one really say that, in Winnicott's terms, it had been good enough?

> The good-enough mother … starts off with an almost complete adaptation to her infant's needs, and as time proceeds she adapts less and less completely, gradually according to the infant's growing ability to deal with her failure. (Winnicott, 1971: 12)

The quotation touches on the imperfection of any human mothering. Perfection, he says elsewhere, is only possible for machines, and in fact is not what is necessary.

> The mother's eventual task is gradually to disillusion the infant, but she has no hope of success unless at first she has been able to give sufficient opportunity for illusion. (Ibid.: 13)

Susan's mother seems to have used her daughter for her own narcissistic needs. How she treated her in infancy we can only guess. She probably clung to the baby as all she had when her husband left. Later, with other means to hand for gratification, she neglected Susan to the extent of letting her be sexually abused and frightened by at least one of her lovers. Later still, her need for Susan returned and increased as she became old and depressed. There was no timely separation. Susan was used (and used herself) as an extension of Mother, and allowed no life of her own. No wonder she mourned the only existence she had ever had.

It was the counsellor's task to help Susan to look closely at her mother's behaviour and accept the ways in which she had been let down, while, at the same time, mourning the good times they had often had together. She needed also, if possible, to build up Susan's self-esteem, and, going back to childhood, discover what, when she 'worked hard' at school, had interested her most. When she looked round art galleries in Italy, had she, for instance, ever felt an urge to do some painting herself? With the assets of enough money and a house, either to live in or sell, all sorts of new possibilities were open to her – if only she could be persuaded it was not too late. As for transference, her dependence would diminish once she became aware of resources in herself. But it was likely to take a long time.

I have been describing Susan's case from a psychodynamic point of view, but I feel confident that much could be done through other imaginative processes, such as visualisations or art therapy. Dependence on the counsellor would still be of extreme relevance – followed by compassionate weaning – even if transference was not defined. Susan's mourning was more complicated than Michael's, as it entailed, at a late age, an about-turn of her whole life-style and the unfamiliar experience of living in accordance with her own wants and needs – once she had recognised what these were – and at last the realisation that she had no one other than herself to live for.

Other difficult cases are those denied bereavements where the mourner persists in refusing to acknowledge grief. This may be seen as courage, but it is more likely that such a person is afraid of the intensity of feeling that must be avoided at all costs, even though the actual cost of this refusal may be all the greater for having been denied. An easy way out is alcohol, or those tranquillisers which doctors are too often happy to hand out, perhaps without realising how much they are colluding with their patients' denial. Or there may be physical symptoms, fears and strange behaviours, seemingly unrelated to the bereavement. Grief, whether denied or accepted, is debilitating. Those newly widowed are usually exceptionally tired. Often they lose sleep and ask for medication without being aware of how addicted they may become. Sometimes the avoidance is deliberate; there are urgent tasks to be done or a determination not to break down in front of one's children. But eventually, as I have already emphasised, the feelings have to be experienced and lived through.

Diminishment

There are a lot of partial deaths before the final exit. Body cells are dying and renewing themselves day by day, but, as the body ages, this renewal becomes less efficient. There is a slowing down of physical activity; hair loses its colour, the skin wrinkles, hearing and sight need enhancement with spectacles and hearing aids. When these losses are gradual, they are not – anyway at first – particularly difficult to accept. Sudden illness and slow recovery are harder to bear, especially when formerly effortless tasks prove exhausting. It is often hard to admit that help is needed, and hanging on to independence becomes all important.

Loss of bodily organs through surgery makes a particular impact. A cancer patient, who had a radical mastectomy, wrote in her diary:

> They tell me I'm lucky. After all it might have been much worse. It was only a spare part. But that's not what I feel. I've lost a bit of me and I don't feel complete without it.

She needed therapy to come to terms with her loss. She was angry – with the surgeon for mutilating her body, with God for giving her cancer, and, guiltily, with her husband, who, while assuring her that it made no difference to his love for her, seemed not to appreciate what she had lost. Her therapist understood that she had wanted her husband to mourn with her, but perhaps he had not dared risk any negative feelings that might come up. She recovered her vitality but felt she had been given a foretaste of mortality.

When there has been a series of bodily diminshments, their cumulative effect can bring such a lowering of self-image and self-esteem that the ensuing depression cannot easily be shaken off. The following illustration shows the effect of multiple losses on a woman in her late 70s.

Diana

Diana was referred by a neighbour who had watched this client's almost complete withdrawal from social life after a failed cataract operation. She agreed reluctantly to see a counsellor. 'Things can only get worse,' was her opening remark. 'There's nothing you can do to help me see properly, ease my arthritis or bring down my blood pressure.' At every session she brought a new complaint. There seemed no illness that she had not suffered from and her whole attention was turned inwards to check what was going on inside her body. 'I'm boring you', she commented and fell into a sullen silence.

It was uncomfortable being with her and she knew it. She was too proud to inflict herself on the few friends and acquaintances that were left, and preferred the companionship of her aged cat, who like her, had lost his looks and was blind in one eye. It turned out that Diana had been blonde and glamorous and, as she put it, 'had the world at my feet'. But she had thrown away her chances of happiness as not being good enough to satisfy her. She had hoped to marry a celebrity, preferably a millionaire, but found herself with an ordinary but long-suffering husband, whom she despised and never mourned when he died. They had no children. 'I'm a wreck,' she declared. 'Nobody cares what happens to me. Nobody wants to know me.'

'There's your neighbour,' said the counsellor, 'who cared enough to worry about you.' It became clear that what Diana was avoiding was any kind of emotional involvement with other people. Too many friends had died. Others, she said, had 'dumped' her. She saw herself as a miserable old woman and there was no point in being alive. But she continued to monitor her bodily functions as if trying to control them. It seemed that she feared seizing up altogether. 'When my cat dies, I'll go too.' Often she admitted to wanting death, yet would shudder and say she was afraid. 'Of life, or death?' asked the counsellor.

'Both.'

She could be honest with her counsellor and sometimes they shared a wry joke, but her zest for life was not restored. She continued with the counselling as her only way of being in touch with a world outside her own body and that of her cat, but would never admit to getting anything out of it. The counsellor felt a failure but went on seeing her. The cat died and her caring neighbour found her a kitten. Diana lived on for the kitten's sake, and showed glimpses, for the first time in her life of maternal tenderness, even though she denied feeling anything at all.

Diana might be said to suffer from what Jung called 'loss of soul', by which he meant losing one's way on the road to finding meaning in one's life, an alienation from one's true self, and a loss of purpose. In Diana's case, worn down by age, disillusion and bodily diminishment, she was not prepared to risk further suffering by struggling to find a more purposeful way to live – though there was, perhaps, a gleam of hope in nurturing a newborn, helpless kitten, with whose fragility she could identify. The counsellor tried to show her that the kitten could be a symbol of new birth and hope for herself, but Diana refused to respond to what she called a 'ridiculous fantasy'. Although near to despair, she did not finally succumb but could hang on to some shred of integrity, at least as a survivor, who no longer reached towards narcissistic goals. It was hard also for her counsellor not to get contaminated by the very stagnent water in which Diana so often seemed to wallow, but to hang on to all that was meaningful in her own life.

Loss of self

Without going into a philosophical dissertation on a definition of 'self', I would like to concentrate on what it feels like to lose control of whatever we are accustomed to regard as our identity, our 'me'. At a certain age, which varies enormously from one individual to another, we become aware, sometimes as a shock, more often through a slow fading, that our familiar selves are changing.

> What will the next deficit be? How will we cope? How will death come? How much life is left to us? All these thoughts lead to varying degrees of fear, the wish to discuss such matters and to deny such thoughts. There may be an increased concern, an over-interest in personal health; or judgements may be set against the age of parental death, and the survival of brothers and sisters. (Scrutton, 1995: 12)

Old people learn to live with a certain amount of pain. What is more alarming is the disorientation and forgetfulness that assails them, often when least expected. They forget the names of their best friends or suddenly an ordinary word is unavailable. They lose pieces of paper, address books, cheques. They forget the day of the week; sometimes they even forget where they are. The obvious advice is, 'Don't worry – it will come back' – which it usually does, but only when whatever it was is not needed any more. Humour helps, and getting together with ageing friends and realising that one is not alone in one's strangeness. But there is always the fear of getting worse and losing one's 'marbles' altogether, in fact the loss of what one has got used to regarding as 'self'. Other bereavements may be sadder, but losing oneself is probably the most frightening. Is it the counsellor's job to reassure to the extent of denying that the loss is real? Sometimes a client can be more reassured by honesty than denial. One old lady said to her therapist – 'Are you calling me a scatterbrain?' The reply was 'Is that what they called you as a child?' 'Oh yes, all the time.' They were both able to laugh and the old lady said it was practical things that had been most easily forgotten and, in childhood, she used to retort that she had more important topics to think about. 'Perhaps that is still true', said the therapist.

Dementia

Amy

I should like to begin this section by describing some sessions with an old lady who showed signs of being on her way to dementia but the counsellor did not write her off as unsuitable. Amy was 93, living in a nursing home. Her marriage had been described as abusive. She had four children. It was one of her sons who contacted SAGE Counselling Service. I shall give the story in the counsellor's own words.

First she introduces herself: I am Tricia. At SAGE, I work with four very unique and individual clients. My philosophy and approach is humanistically based. I am trained in an integrative approach, that of person-centred, gestalt, and the comparative model of psychodynamic.

The client's son wrote to me and gave me some of the family history, which I initially felt wasn't necessary. After having some telephone supervision, I made contact with the nursing home to introduce myself and arrange my visiting time. We agreed on a Wednesday afternoon in August. I asked the member of staff, 'Please remind my client.' The response was, 'Not necessary. She'll never remember. She's got senile dementia. That's why she's here.' I was surprised as I had not been told this by my client's son.

First Visit: My agenda: anxious because I was unsure about the client's acceptance of me. It was her son who had requested a counsellor. I arrived at three minutes to two. My client knew I was coming! A sense of relief. She is a tall lady, who has some ability to walk without support for short distances.

Touch: She shook my hand and invited me to sit down. She began chatting – some I could understand and a great deal I could not make sense of. I offered her patience, used a great deal of facial and body eye contact and worked in a Rogerian way.

She told me her husband beat her. She loved cricket. She spoke of her children. She did not want to be in the Home. When words failed her, she looked at me. I met her eyes and sensed her initial fear, anger and deep pain. She nodded and smiled. I came away feeling I had made a good beginning. I had also written down the date and time of my next visit and this pleased her.

Second Visit: She recognised me. My perception of her this time was that her phrasing and sentences were flowing more easily and made sense. She spoke more about her love of cricket and showed me a newspaper with a picture of the English team. I again wrote down the date and time of my next visit.

Third Visit: I continued to learn her language.

Fourth Visit: She spoke of her son's wedding. Fifteen minutes into the session, tears rolled down her cheek. She said, 'I'm talking nonsense. I know I am.' The tears rolled. She looked at me and said, 'You know if you give me time, I'll waddle and get there in the end.' I said 'Yes' and nodded. We sat in silence. She sighed, still tearful. I felt moved by her, and my gut response was to go to her, crouch down in front of her and touch her hand. Another sigh. She mopped up her tears and told me I was special for what I do. I thanked her and arranged our next visit.

Fifth Visit: The wedding. I was shown photos and told who was in them. Sometimes her words were incoherent. I told her to take her time. She couldn't understand where her son was. She became agitated, talked of God, Jesus and death. I asked if she was worried about her own death. 'No' – a very quick response. 'No, no, it will be a relief to me. No more worries or arguments.' I reflected back. Her son had wanted me to work on her death.

Sixth Visit: My client was very tired when I arrived. She had told the nursing staff to ring me. (They had not done so.) 'Sorry you had to come all this way.' What she wanted now was peace, no more arguments. I understood. Her words: 'You have been good. I don't want to be rude.' I reflected back, 'You're telling me you don't want me to come any more.' 'Yes, sorry, sorry.' I accepted her decision. She said, 'I understand about Jesus and God. Why can't I just be?' I then left.

Amy was confused and knew that what she said did not always make sense. Unfortunately the nursing staff could only see her as demented and would not bother to convey messages to and from the counsellor. Clearly her son was worried about her being depressed and frightened. Tricia expected to explore her fear of death but, when Amy opened up the subject, it was to say that death would be more welcome than frightening. Perhaps the fear belonged more to her son than to herself. What I find worrying about this story is the way the carers took it for granted that her confusion was dementia, an attitude that is bound to discourage old people from trying to express themselves. My advice to counsellors is always to show respect for their elderly clients and to realise that treating them as more lucid than they actually are does no harm, whereas talking down or ignoring them causes unnecessary distress. It is often surprising how much sense one can find even in confused conversation, if one takes the trouble to listen. Amy's use of the word 'waddle' was quite an apt way of describing her efforts to convey what she wanted to say.

Can counselling help dementia patients?

The answer appears, surprisingly, to be yes – especially in the early stages when a person may be aware of what is happening and have some idea of what a bleak future lies ahead. People feel guilty, as though memory loss is their fault and they are responsible for their own brains. This guilt is an important issue for counsellors, whose clients need to stop blaming themselves. The fault is not with the self but with the neural transmitter, a vital piece of machinery that is letting its owner down.

Some would argue that the brain is the self: 'Dementia reflects the deterioration and decay of the person or self' (Gilleard, 1984: 10). Others regard the demented as prisoners in their failing bodies. Jungians might see the power of the unconscious taking over as the seat of consciousness (the brain) loses its functions. As I hope to illustrate, personalities still manage to express themselves, even when the disease progresses, although communication is not easy and not every counsellor, however well-trained or experienced, will succeed in getting through to a dementing client, though some seem to have a natural talent, as for instance, this priest: 'I often find that with the confused you can chat heart to heart. You can touch people where we really come together' (Butler and Orbach, 1993: 153). I take him to mean that communication is simplified. One does not put on an act; one is not trying to impress, any more than one does with a baby at the pre-verbal stage. Eye contact and smiles may be more effective than words.

Elizabeth Bartlett, from the Salisbury Alzheimer's Disease Society, has done some counselling with dementia sufferers and is able to give some practical advice. She has often found that a walk in the open air may be easier than sitting in a room face to face. Silence may be more easily accepted out of doors; one needs to learn to tolerate silence and to remember that only 7 per cent of human communication is verbal. The counsellor must not generalise; each dementing person is unique and one needs to adapt and get to know the individual, whose previous history should, if possible, be studied and referred to in the counselling. Remember that dementia is only a small part of the client's life-story. The counsellor should talk clearly, using short sentences. If the client does not understand, rather than repeating oneself, she advises rephrasing, using different words, very much in the same way as one would with a foreigner, learning the language. Keep it simple and avoid jumping from one subject to another. Don't use open-ended questions, such as, for instance, 'what do you want to do?' instead of 'do you want to go for a walk?' Making choices is hard when logic is impaired. When the client's talk is hard to understand, she advises being honest. But, instead of saying bluntly, 'I don't know what you mean,' try making a guess – 'do you mean … ?' Events long past may be talked about as happening now, or the talk may be about what never actually happened but the client wished it had. There will be confabulation – inventing stories to compensate for loss of memory.

In trying to empathise with a client's demented world, one might conjure up an image of driving through a fog that hardly ever clears, though there may be tantalising glimpses of how things used to be; or think of riding a bicycle backwards and getting nowhere; it is uphill all the way, confusing and frustrating.

Working with dementia nevertheless bring some refreshing surprises. John Killick writes as a poet who delights in the poetic potential he has discovered in some of these sufferers, whom he has visited regularly in a residential home. He has put together what amounts to an anthology, in which he explains that it came about as a result of co-operative work between these residents and himself. He listens carefully to what is said and writes it down unchanged. His selection gives the words poetic form, though, in no case, was the subject consciously attempting poetry. Killick (1994) maintains that, contrary to expectations, people with dementia do not use language 'stripped to the functional', but their words produce images, for instance, describing rain: 'I wish it could wring it out of its system.' And on old-age: 'The finishing days are here.'

He pays attention to a person's body language, which sometimes tells him as much as the words used. Sentences may be scrambled, so attention to body and tone of voice may be his only means of interpreting. He has learnt to respond quickly to mood changes and whether his subject needs physical reassurance such as holding hands. He needs to keep his concentration. Any wandering of his own attention will impede making sense of what he hears. He is aware that the whole exercise can cause distress; hidden memories surface and bring strong emotions. The effort of communicating may provoke tears of frustration. He needs to share these reactions with the nursing staff, but also to respect his subjects' confidences. The following verses show how he made a poem from what one of these residents was saying:

> I'm suffering from monkey-puzzle.
> The monkey-puzzle is this place.
> The puzzle is how to cope with the monkeys...
> It's a rum do, this growing ancient.
> The brilliance of my brain
> has slipped away
> while I wasn't looking. (Killick, 1994: 3)

Another resident sums up her life-story: 'You climb the family tree and see the vista from there.' Killick (1994) comments that she 'thus encapsulates in a sentence the theory behind life-history work with elderly people.'

Killick is not a counsellor, but his listenening and the way he orders what he hears may give counsellors a new insight into the usually closed world of dementia.

Reflection and review

I suggest using the following questions to test your capacity for empathy, by putting yourself, as far as possible, in your client's place.

- Imagine your retirement. How will you plan for it? Do you think it will worry you having to organise your days without a set timetable?
- Imagine a client being made redundant suddenly. What sort of counselling help do you think he most needs?
- You are counselling a woman of 80, who feels she has missed out on life through never having had children. She minds this more, not less, in her old age. How might you help this client to feel she has some stake in the future?
- Imagine yourself in the position of caring for a partner or close relative with dementia. What help do you think you would seek for yourself – befriending (with hugs and cups of tea) or in-depth counselling? Or neither?
- What would you say to a client who asks if you have noticed that her memory is going, and wants to know if you think she has Alzheimer's?

10

Facing Death

Counselling older people must involve opening our minds to the reality of death. For those of us in mid-life, immersed in everything to do with living, it is perhaps hard to grasp that clients, parents, partners, and eventually we, ourselves, all have to die. We do of course know it as a fact, but have we allowed ourselves to think about it? If we are not prepared to accept the inevitability of our own dying, perhaps we should think twice about taking on clients in an older age group.

I suggest sitting still for a few minutes and imagining yourself terminally ill, unable to control the future. Are you afraid that you will not be able to bear the pain, that it will inevitably get worse? Can you trust those who care for you to alleviate some of your suffering? Are you afraid of dying alone? Think about who you would most like to confide in about how you feel – your doctor, your vicar, a counsellor? Consider those whom you have to leave behind, the goodbyes that need to be said. Will you be able to talk openly to those nearest to you, your partner, your children? You may need to forgive and be forgiven, to make peace with friends, with yourself or with God. Think how this can best be done. Perhaps the hardest of all is having to live with uncertainty, and having to accept that neither you, nor those who care for you, can do anything to change your fate. Can you face what is happening without trying to fight against it? What, to your mind, is a good death? If we can ask these questions of ourselves, we should be better able to listen to the hopes and fears of those who are likely to be nearer to dying than we are. Being able to think about one's own death may make it seem a bit more familiar – a bit more known. But we also need to be aware of individual differences in approach.

At a weekend workshop, participants were encouraged to voice their beliefs about death. One had attended a spiritualist church and received a message from his dead brother – 'So of course there's a spirit world'. Others described 'near death experiences' as moving down a tunnel towards a light. Or there was comfort in a life well lived and in being able to say one had done one's best. Some were consoled by having children and grandchildren to live after them, or they spoke of a cycle of deaths and births; at each death, there is a birth and life begins for someone else. Our bodies would be recycled and made into compost to enrich the physical world. There might be a part of us called 'soul' but most of the participants did not think of it as immortal. To each statement, the facilitator would say:

'That's your truth, but listen to the others.' So each made a contribution and there was no argument.

In the childhood of some of our clients, it was sex that could only be mentioned in whispers. Later the taboo was death. A nurse was told:

> I was never to mention the subject even if the patient asked, nor was I to speak about it to any relatives, no matter what the situation. I witnessed some appalling deaths. We were allowed to lay out their bodies but we were not allowed to talk about it. (Letter to the Natural Death Centre – Albery, Elliot and Elliot, 1977: 23)

At last things are changing. Doctors even find it possible to tell their patients they are going to die, though many do so with great reluctance because they still seem to think of each death as a medical failure, which it is their job to avoid. 'The Hippocratic oath has been taken to absurd lengths' (Scrutton, 1995: 28). So, although doctors these days are less likely to tell their patients lies, the truth may be told awkwardly. I know a case of the doctor asking his patient if she had come alone – which she clearly had – and then blurting our that her cancer was invasive and she had only a few years to live. After operating, it was found that the cancer had not spread and there was no confirmation of its invasiveness. Fortunately there had been a counselling nurse attached to the unit, who had helped the patient to cope with the doctor's devastating prognosis. Afterwards, he modified his words.

Counsellors need to show themselves willing to talk to their clients about death, but it is sometimes difficult to know when, and if, this is wanted. In the last chapter, we saw how Amy's counsellor had been warned by the client's brother that this was an area that she (or he?) was wanting to explore. The counsellor was ready, only to find that her client's attitude to death was that it would be a 'relief'. I would say that, in each case, we need first to build a trusting relationship and, once this is established, it may, in fact, be quite easy to ask the client about fear and regret at having to die. Unless we show ourselves ready to talk about it, the client may be wary about mentioning the subject, purely out of courtesy to the counsellor, who – so the client thinks – may be wanting to avoid it.

We need also to realise that the dying person's awareness comes and goes, as if too much of it would be overwhelming. John Hinton describes this fluctuating knowledge:

> She did not always want to admit that she was dying. In subsequent conversations, in spite of her earlier awareness of the true nature of her illness, she would often speak in a light wondering fashion about her symptoms, as if she could not begin to guess what caused them. There were times when she wanted to maintain this pretence with others and not refer to her real state. (Hinton, 1990: 12)

Another way of protection is to confine all thought to everyday happenings in the relative safety of the sick room, where life is monotonously peaceful and punctuated by routines of meals, medicaments and the changing shifts of nurses. People send cards, bring flowers and relay items of news from a wider world. But visitors are not welcomed if they are full of chat and are too obviously avoiding any mention of the invalid's impending death. I remember a case where the hospital chaplain came to say prayers, a friend read poetry and a third visitor sat in silence by the bed. Counsellors are used to silences and should be aware of those that are appropriate at such moments and those that might be frightening. Only by allowing silence can we allow the initiative to come from the dying person, whether in important (perhaps even last) words or (beyond words) in a change of facial expression, perhaps a smile.

It is, however, not very likely that the counsellor finds herself in the position of being present at the moment of death. The readiness should be there and, if it happens, she may regard it as a privilege. But it is more probable that she will have handed over her responsibility to a team of those professionals – doctors, nurses, chaplains – who are trained, and who expect, to cope with those who die. It may be hard for the counsellor to have to make this surrender, feeling perhaps not yet ready to take her leave. It is harder still to hear no further news from relatives, who may not even have known about the old person's counselling. Usually, someone will break the news of the actual death, but not the details. If the counsellor decides to attend the funeral, it will be anonymously, sitting at the back and slipping away after the service.

Stage theory

Elizabeth Kübler-Ross (1970) asserted that a patient's emotional response to terminal illness moved through five recognisable stages: denial, anger, bargaining (with God?), depression, and finally acceptance. She came to this conclusion after intensive work with dying people, listening to them and watching their reactions. Tony Walter, in his sociological study of 20th century dying, makes this comment:

> Her meta-story is one many want to hear. Her message is that so long as carers do not engage in conspiracies of silence, so long as they let the patient be and express feelings, then death is not to be feared – patients will naturally progress to the final peaceful stage of acceptance. (Walter, 1994: 71)

Although Kübler-Ross has admitted that not everyone goes through all five stages, or not necessarily in the same order, her 'meta-story' has caught on and been learnt by hundreds of medical students, nurses and carers, who have sometimes welcomed it as a simplification of the dying process – even though it does not, of course, apply to sudden death. Walter argues that stage theory can also get in the way of actual listening to what dying people are saying. The theory can be helpful if not adhered to rigidly, but can too easily be misused, both as regards dying and, as I have already suggested, in helping the bereaved. 'Whether applied to dying or bereaved persons, categories such as denial and anger have the potential to be both an aid to listening and a short-cut that cuts out true listening'

(Ibid.: 76). This is a warning against generalisations. Counsellors need to respect how diverse are individual ways of coping. That is why it is helpful to monitor reactions to one's own death and compare them with those of colleagues or fellow students.

Fear of dying

Some fear of the process must be almost universal. With slow, wasting disease and the body's gradual disintegration it becomes impossible to keep up stratagems of denial. This painful reality is what people in favour of euthanasia seek to avoid. Those who die unexpectedly from sudden heart attacks are usually considered lucky. But others feel they would like some warning, so that they can set their affairs in order and say their goodbyes. In the days when people unconditionally believed in heaven and hell, a good death was the one that came slowly, giving time for the dying person to prepare. Beliefs have changed and become vaguer. Life after death may only seem real as continuing in our descendants and in people's memories. The prolongation of dying gives time for a gradual withdrawal from worldly values and offers a chance for the process of non-attachment to the usual joys that have seemed to make life worth living. This is not easy but realistic when the fight for life becomes useless. A voluntary giving up may dispel some of the fear.

Fear of death

> When one is alone and it is night and so dark and still that one hears nothing and sees nothing but the thoughts which add and subtract the years, and the long row of those disagreeable facts which remorselessly indicate how far the hand of the clock has moved forward and the slow irresistible approach of the wall of darkness which will eventually engulf everything I love, possess, wish for, hope for, then all our profundities about life slink off to some undiscoverable hiding lace, and fear envelops the sleepless one like a smothering blanket. (Jung, 1977: 405)

Jung gives such a clear description of his fear that any who have felt it themselves are bound to recognise him as a fellow sufferer, although, as an old man, he showed every sign of coming to terms with it, as any reading of his autobiographical *Memories, Dreams, Reflections* (1967) will show. In fact, he tended to refer to death as life's eventual goal (1967, 1990).

It is often said that children are not afraid of death because they don't know what it is, or don't consider it permanent, or because they think of it as only happening to old people, and they are immune. This may be true of children who have been well loved and brought up in a stable environment that enabled them to build a solid sense of self. If they feel shaky about who they are and are not well established in life, there is likely to be uneasiness and a sense of impending loss when their lives and selves are, in any way, threatened. I suggest that this can also apply to the very old, whose sense of self is crumbling, both physically and through increasing memory loss. It also becomes realistic to be afraid of death as something that is going to happen to them in the near future, about which they can know nothing for certain, although sometimes the closer they are, the less they seem to be afraid.

Kate

Kate, aged 85, was a client who was slow to mention her fear of death as something that had haunted her for most of her life. She talked about the deaths of other people: her father, who had been killed in the first World War, too early for her to remember him, her husband, her brother and, very sadly, her only son who, aged five, had been at a friend's house when it got bombed, so he was a casualty of the second World War. When her husband came home from service overseas, they had two daughters about whom she was always anxious. When they were growing up, she kept watch over all their movements and sat up waiting for them to come home from parties. She made it difficult for them to leave home. Even now, when they were both married with families of their own, she expected daily bulletins recounting all the things they did, and she was critical of the way they brought up their children, letting them do what they liked in a dangerous world – 'where anything could happen'.

Her counsellor was a man of 40. She had asked for a man. She told him that he was the age her son would have been and he managed not to correct her. She hated people to grow old, found it hard to believe in her own ageing and was worried by rapid change in what was becoming an unfamiliar world. The counsellor reflected back her hatred of change and added, 'You need to have everything under your control'. She seemed not to take this in, but, next time they met, she said, 'I suppose we ought to be talking about death' and gave a shudder. The counsellor was taken aback, but suggested, 'Is that what you're avoiding?' Then he added, 'Perhaps it's what we're both avoiding.'

'Oh yes. When I'm here with you, it's all right, but alone at night, it can be terrifying – the nothingness of it.'

'Nothingness? Has your life really meant nothing?'

'I'm not religious, so it all ends in nothing.' Her counsellor remembered Erikson's stages of life as a series of opposite possibilities, the last of these being generativity versus despair (Erikson, 1959). He had also read Frankl's *Man's Search for Meaning* (1987). By concentrating on life instead of death, and showing interest in the life-story of this particular client, he encouraged her to reminisce and give her story a shape before letting go of it altogether. She did not feel like writing it down for her family to read, only to understand it herself, share it with this counsellor, who seemed so like a son, and give it some sort of meaning. She admitted that she had tried to control her children, but said she had done this out of love. They were precious and she had been afraid of losing them. But, the more she tried to keep them with her, the more they got away. 'And now they want to control me – by putting me in an institution.' The counsellor suggested that this too might be because they loved and wanted to protect her, but she found that hard to believe. There seemed to be a breakdown of communication. What initiative could she take to put this right? How could she show her love?

There was a long pause before she managed to say, 'By giving'.

'What could you give?'

'Books, pictures, jewellery. I might find out who wants what, now before I die, and hope there won't be arguments afterwards.' What else, he wondered, could she give. Memories perhaps, not just her own but being able to add to theirs – their childhood memories. It might be interesting to compare their separate versions of the past. She could tell them about a time before they were born, work out a family tree, so that she could see herself, and each one of them, as part of history.

Before the planned end of their counselling, Kate had a stroke and was left partly paralysed but she could still talk. She asked her counsellor to visit her in hospital and they had a last 'session' with him setting by her bed. She was able to say how kind and loving her daughters had been and that one of them had offered to give her a home in the new house she was buying. Kate was amazed to find she was actually wanted. 'You gave us all a fright,' her daughter had said, 'and we don't want to lose you.' The counsellor asked about her fear of death. 'I suppose I've begun dying already – bit by bit – and so far it's all right. You see – I don't feel so alone.'

She was able, quite easily, to let her counsellor go, and he felt, to his relief, less like a son. She squeezed his hand. 'But I want you to remember me.' He assured her that he would.

Euthanasia

We should not assume that all old people want to live. Many do not dread death as much as the misery of going on with a greatly reduced quality of a life, without dignity or purpose, of being a burden to others and also to themselves. Like Kate, they want to be in control of their lives, but theirs is a different kind of control, a different avoidance. They have looked death in the face and acknowledged its certainty, but, since death cannot be avoided, they believe that they should be allowed at least to choose its time and setting. Their fear is focused, not on death as non-being, but on the process of dying, either in pain or in an uncontrollable, demented state.

Since euthanasia is illegal, they may choose to commit suicide while they are still physically and mentally strong enough to act on that decision.

One of the easiest ways is to refuse food in the hope that this will be understood as their choice, without having the food forced upon them.

What, in such stressful circumstances, can a counsellor do to help? Professionally, there is no action possible, nor is there much to be gained by attempting to argue the client out of what is often, not a panic reaction, but a carefully considered decision. It is not, as all counsellors know, their job to give advice, but, in this sort of crisis, it is surely worth drawing the client's attention to the legality of an 'advance directive', or, as it is often called, 'living will', which sets out in writing the circumstances in which this person would want to refuse any treatment aimed at prolonging life. The list covers such diseases as incurable cancer, degeneration of the nervous system, severe brain damage and dementia. The document is signed and witnessed in the same way as the usual legal will, bequeathing money and possessions. Doctors today are no longer looked up to as having the power to decide when to resuscitate cases of cardiac arrest in very old people without having first discovered the will of the patient and that of the nearest relative. In such cases, an advance directive is obviously helpful, though the difficulty remains that the patient who has become unable to speak for himself, may, when it comes to this point, have changed his attitude. How can anyone know for certain what goes on in his (or her) enfeebled mind? An important point is that the judgement should not be based on a person's age but on the severity of the medical condition. There is no question of the doctor killing the patient, merely of letting nature run its course, and, in many cases of terminal illness, patients are able to give their consent before complete helplessness sets in.

It seems unlikely that a counsellor will be asked to put these choices to the person concerned, though counselling, in such circumstances, may help the relatives, as they struggle to come to terms with a decision to withdraw life support or stop feeding. The counsellor would be able to show them that their feelings can, in fact, make a difference, that they have every right to stand up to the medical authorities and assert whatever convictions they may hold on the sanctity of life. One could also argue that the counsellor might appropriately have a place on the medical and nursing team that meets to discuss these life and death choices.

Religious consolation

We have got used to seeing church pews full of old people who still, we think, retain the beliefs instilled in them during childhood, without noticing that a change is taking place. This is another reminder (and there are plenty) that today's 'oldies' are not the same people who were old when we were young. According to a recent survey of religious attitudes, a 68 year-old man had this to say:

> It now seems intellectually preposterous to me to maintain that there is a personal God who can alter actions as a result of prayer. I can no longer see any reason at all to think there's a life after death, even though death is getting closer. (*The Observer*, 3/9/00)

Not only irrelevant church services but lack of pastoral care from the clergy seem to be factors people mention as driving them away from regular worship. The fact that they are bringing some of their problems to counselling rather than to church should at least persuade us to listen and accept what our clients are saying, and stay with the mystery and uncertainty without fobbing them off with conventional images of things beyond our ken.

Staying with what a client says sometimes proves difficult for those counsellors who have strong religious beliefs themselves, who maintain that there is only one way to God, and see it as their duty to evangelise. Supervisors need to be extra vigilant in seeing that such people develop an ability to keep their opinions out of the room, and become simply mirrors to reflect back what their clients are saying. Many clients, we find, have a belief in God, even if none in the Church. In one case that I remember, a counsellor was seeing an old lady near to death, who was afraid because she had no beliefs, only doubts. The counsellor's faith was strong and the client knew this and wanted it given to her. They worked quietly together for some time, but the counsellor was not tempted to persuade or convert. Yet, somehow, her faith supported the client who lost her fear. There was a mutual decision to end, but the client died peacefully before the last session.

Reflection and review

- As a counsellor, you may have feelings of much sadness on hearing about your client's death. You want perhaps to attend the funeral. Do you think this would be appropriate?
- An elderly client has a life-long fear of death, a fear of non-being. What positive help do you think you could give? Would you find it difficult just to stay with this client and acknowledge your own helplessness?
- How would you cope with breaking the news to a terminally ill patient that no more can be done to save his or her life?
- Think about what has been depicted as a 'good death', both historically and today. Notice how people's views have changed. This would be a good topic to discuss in a group of colleagues. What would you like to say to the group? Can you voice your opinions honestly and openly?

11

How do we Evaluate Counselling?

Since Eysenck gave his negative judgement in 1952, 50 years of research into counselling and psychotherapy have come up with the verdict – yes, counselling does work, (Burton, 1998, Wiener and Sher, 1993) but there is considerable disagreement about which model suits which patient, the length of treatment required and how it should be evaluated. As for differences between counselling models, research shows that they all work equally.

The available literature has almost nothing to say about counselling older people, who, if mentioned at all, tend to be side-lined, along with ethnic minorities, as unlikely to benefit. Surveys indicate that 10–20 per cent of old people suffer from depression (Burton, 1998), which often goes undetected or is given a low priority by referrers. Some regions have no services for this often neglected age group; others have specialised geriatric units. Our ageing population poses new problems in all walks of life, not least in the mental health of our older citizens. The old should no longer be regarded as a silent minority. I have heard of at least one research project set up to explore old-age counselling, but it is as yet too early for any results to be forthcoming.

Before counselling services became professionalised and burgeoned into a 'growth industry', success or failure would have been appraised by client satisfaction and supervisory approval, together with a careful assessment of each client's potential and what was likely to be achieved in a course of therapy. Length of treatment was not the issue it has now become, and clients were expected to stay for 'as long as it takes', unless the inexperienced counsellor failed to relate and, as a result, 'lost' the client after a few sessions. Therapy was thus open-ended and dependency on the counsellor a problem that was not to be strenuously avoided but worked through.

It is with the acceptance of therapy as efficacious treatment and its absorption into NHS primary care, that pressure has been put on the profession to give value for money and to submit to complicated evaluation processes in order to discover the quickest and least expensive means of achieving that end. One inevitable result has been a certain amount of medical domination. Treatment must be seen to be scientific. Clients (patients) have to be 'diagnosed', their symptoms spelt out, their 'diseases' given names. Three kinds of outcome are looked for:

(1)   clinical – showing a drop in symptom level and an improved quality of life
(2)   medical utilisation – a drop in consultation rate or use of inpatient facilities
(3)   patient satisfaction (a satisfied customer) (Burton, 1998: 189).

It is interesting that patient satisfaction is listed as the lowest priority.

Quantitative or qualitative research

There has been much debate about these two approaches, as shown in the following table (McLeod, 1998: 324):

Qualitative	Quantitative
Description and interpretation of meanings	Measurement and analysis of variables
Quality of relationship between researcher and informants important	Aims for neutral, objective relationship
Necessity for self-awareness and reflexivity in researcher	Aims for value-free researcher
Uses interviews, participant observation, diaries	Uses tests, rating scales, questionnaires
Researcher(s) interpret data	Statistical analysis of data
Strongest in sociology, social anthropology, theology and the arts	Strongest in psychology and psychiatry
Many similar ideas to psychoanalysis and humanistic therapies	Many similar ideas to behavioural and cognitive therapies

This table shows that there is a gap to be bridged between what can and cannot be quantified, between medical and interpretive thinking and whether counselling is an applied science or more akin to practising an art.

Typical of the quantitative (medical) approach is the Randomised Control Trial (RCT) for demonstrating the efficacy of psychotherapy. Therapists are trained and supervised to administer a model which has been set out in a manual. Adherence to the manual is regularly monitored and 'useful' interventions noted. Clients chosen for this research must have a single disorder, having been screened for comorbidity. They are then randomly assigned for treatment. RCTs show:

> what works for whom in the most ideal set of circumstances, delivered by the most ideal practitioners to the most ideal patients with the most ideal specificity and severity of problem. (Mellor-Clark, 1997, quoted by Burton, 1998: 164)

Cognitive and behavioural practitioners may be happy with RCTs, but psychodynamic and humanistic counsellors are likely to see weaknesses in a method that simplifies the multiple problems presented by most of their clients, with the assumption that a single disorder can be isolated. Counsellor and client may choose to focus on a particular problem but what the researchers call comorbidity can hardly be ignored. Most counsellors would agree that curing symptoms has less relevance to their practice than a general improvement in the client's well-being and creative use of new experience. In using a manual, the relationship between counsellor and client (therapist and patient) tends to be dismissed. It is as though individuals are being reduced to statistics. Assignment of treatment depends on throwing together all those with the same diagnosis, regardless of cultural differences, previous experience and other variations. Counsellors trained in integretive therapy may want to choose from different models to suit individual clients. A manualised approach would be seen as greatly restricting their freedom.

The view that manualised therapy, with its standardisation of clinical procedures, ensures that patients receive validated treatment, has been criticised as not guaranteeing competence or benefiting the therapeutic allowance (Henry et al., 1993). 'Therapists who adhered best to treatment guidelines tended to be more controlling, hostile and prone to negative interactions with patients' (Burton, 1998, p: 165). Roth and Fonagy et al. (1996) come out in favour of RCTs as the only valid source of evidence for efficacy of treatment, but admit that their conclusions are limited; data from trials cannot be transferred directly into a clinical context. The UK Deparment of Health takes a cautious view of 'validated' therapy and does not recommend particular treatments for specific diagnoses.

The USA is promoting brief and ultra brief therapies on cost containment grounds, leaving long-term therapies under-researched; yet the general view in the UK today seems to be that, on the whole, more therapy is generally better than less and the more disturbed the client, the harder it is to make therapeutic gains (Burton, 1998: 189–90). Outcome measurement no longer relies on comparing pre- and post-treatment studies but monitors changes throughout the process of therapy. The Psychological Treatment Research Centre (PTRC) at Leeds University has developed a Standardised CORE Outcome Measure, which includes sub-scales for subjective well-being, symptoms, life/social functioning and risk/harm. Clinicians are asked to complete forms at the beginning and end of treatment, whereas their clients must be willing to complete a CORE Measure every six sessions. This procedure 'is a good example of the minimum data-set any primary care service should be collecting' (Ibid.: 190). And we are reminded that 'if you do not evaluate your own service, someone else will do it for you, and use the results for their own political ends' (Ibid.: 191).

We must remember that these procedures belong to treatment provided free on the NHS, as also to US Managed Care, paid for by insurance comanies. In the sphere of treating older people, the young-old may be assessed as suitable for a course of therapy (probably time-limited) but the old-old, who need home or hospital visits, are less likely to be catered for, nor do they constitute particularly appropriate subjects for research, in that long-term follow-up may find them either dead or on their way to dementia and therefore (perhaps) considered not worth the money spent on treating them. This sounds callous and the situation is unlikely to be described in those words, but will nevertheless affect assessment criteria.

Even in private practice, therapists may, as we have seen, be wary about taking on people of an older generation, but there are counselling services with charitable status, some of which (like SAGE), are specially geared for treating older people, and these can be located through local bodies such as Age Concern or Social Services, and will attempt to meet these clients' needs without asking for more than minimum payment, often described as a donation to cover expenses. Any evaluation of such clients will, it is hoped, be sensitive and only undertaken with their full consent and co-operation.

Research as narrative

Known as 'The Talking Cure', the therapeutic process is a conversation. The client tells a story. The counsellor listens and responds. The two participants learn to share a language, and it is in the context of what they share that changes may occur. Some forms of qualitative research involve telling stories. Freud wrote case histories to advance his theories. Counselling students write notes on their sessions and are required to draw on these to compose an extended study on which qualification depends. Further accreditation again relies on insights derived from writing a case history. One could say that all practising therapists/counsellors are researchers, though not in the way of proving to doctors that they have performed cures or even removed symptoms, inexpensively and in the shortest possible time. The story does not set out to prove anything, but, at its best, shows progression from one state of being to another, with the client participating by being able eventually to let go of the counsellor, with enough strength to face life's vicissitudes. With each story submitted for expert criticism, a modicum of research will have been undertaken by showing which counselling interventions have moved the process towards a satisfactory end, and which moments of shared crisis may have suddenly been seen by both counsellor and client as a breakthrough. Although each client is a separate individual, enough generalisation can be inferred (without reducing the person to a statistic) to indicate which theories work, or even occasionally to create new ones.

In the area of qualitative research, the experience of the client has been explored, not only through standardised questionnaires but in intensive interviews after finishing counselling (Maluccio, 1979). Other researchers have concentrated on single sessions to enable clients to re-experience what they thought and felt at the time (Rennie, 1990, 1992), through listening to sessions that have been recorded and are played back with the researcher present, the client stopping the tape at points where particular feelings are remembered. Rennie concludes that clients are responding to their counsellors on different levels. Their feelings are often at odds with what is spoken.

Exploring the clients' world has produced a 'grounded theory', which is 'inductively derived from the study of the phenomenon it represents' (Strauss and Corbin, 1990: 23). This is a theory without any hypothesis formed in advance. Nothing is taken for granted except the observed data.

Grounded theory has been supposed to give qualitative research a solid base and more credibility in the medical establishment, but has been criticised by some in the therapy profession for its assumption of 'an objective reality "out there" that could be viewed and analysed by following clearly defined rules of data collection and analysis' (West, 2001, p. 127). West believes in developing pluralistic approaches to research. He pursues his own heuristic enquiry, a method of finding out what is going on by involving both therapist and client in the exploration. Instead of treating one another as objects he advocates engaging in an I/thou relationship (Buber, 1970). It is our own humanness that enables us to understand other humans. In involving our clients in the research, what we need is a disciplined subjectivity.

It is pointed out that, in collecting data about people, we are never totally objective. Data collection is socially constructed. So we learn that research reports are themselves ways of telling stories. Another writer, Peter Martin (2000), states that he has no intention of producing a theory; his aim is to create an evocative narrative. Both he and Etherington (2000), whose book he reviews, believe that researchers should use themselves – their life-experiences, attitudes, biases – as part of the narrative. Etherington's narrative is multi-layered, being made up of her clients' stories, her own as their counsellor and, in a different character, their researcher, as well as her personal story of being a client and a survivor. In her recent writing (2001), there is self-disclosure, which, at this point, holds no fears for her regarding judgement by colleagues or academics, but she was worried that her clients, in reading about themselves, would learn more about her than is usually considered appropriate. She talked it through with the two clients concerned and found that her disclosures had affected them but not, in the long run, had adverse effects.

There is obviously more to be said about the new directions being taken by qualitative researchers, but my aim here is to see how much, if any, of it, applies to counselling older people, and what answers we are able to give convincingly to the question: 'How do you know that counselling this age group works?'

Referring back to the clients whose stories I have discussed in this book, I would say that few, if any, of them, fit neatly into diagnostic categories. In only one case, that of Michael in Chapter 9, could the therapy be described as 'manualised', in that his counsellor had learnt the stage-theory of bereavement, which she found a useful framework for recognising where she was with her client. Recognition of each expected stage enabled her to feel the therapy was moving in accordance with an established pattern. If Michael had been asked how he saw their progress, he would probably have described it differently, perhaps expressing gratitude to his counsellor for staying with him and believing that he had the strength to invest in a new phase of life. I wonder whether either of them would have acknowledged that the breakthrough came when the counsellor challenged his idealised description of his dead wife, thus bringing reality into the therapy.

Susan (Chapter 9) was going through a more complicated bereavement and her reaction could easily have been labelled pathological. What was needed was long-term treatment to work through her dependency and regression, and relating her present neediness to the somewhat bizarre pattern of her childhood. I doubt if, at 77, she would have been accepted for counselling in primary care. Fortunately, she had the money to pay for private therapy.

Looking at Kate in Chapter 10, do we call fear of death a symptom? The focus could have been on the multiple bereavements of her earlier life to which her fear was obviously linked. The counsellor might have colluded with her avoidance of that fear. Instead, he acknowledged its power, hinting that he also had felt its grip. What eventually made a difference was suddenly, through her stroke, being brought to the brink of death. When she discovered that her daughters loved her and would not leave her to die alone, she was able to let go of both her counsellor and life itself. The medical alternative to counselling would probably have been tranquillising drugs, which, as in so many cases, would have been a financial drain on the NHS, and not at all what the client wanted.

Rachael, in Chapter 5, was not depressed enough to be diagnosed as having an illness. She was reacting to an adjustment in her life-situation which was making her lonely. She needed to find a way of telling her story and, by re-thinking her assumptions, come to understand the separate story of her son. What passed between mother and son was private and could only be evaluated by watching the change in her behaviour and in how she related to the people she encountered every day.

Robin, in Chapter 7, was not ill, unless one takes the outmoded view that homosexuality is an illness to be cured. If that had been the goal, his counselling would have failed. As it was, he was encouraged to 'come out', feel accepted and drop his guilt feelings. Any public 'coming out' was perhaps too much to hope for at 77, but he could learn to feel less persecuted and to recognise a more gay-friendly world than that of his youth.

Perhaps the most obvious success was the case of Mary in Chapter 4. This was time-limited and the goals were reached. This client was also going through a bereavement, this time of a dementing husband. Through her counselling, she was able to let him go and discover new interests.

Much harder to evaluate is the story of Bob, the flood victim, described in Chapter 4. This time the therapy was open-ended. If confined to only a few sessions, his main, psychosomatic symptoms would probably have remained hidden. The presenting problem of the flood turned out to be merely a trigger, reviving panic attacks that had been with him for most of his life, causing him shame as well as fear. It took many months to disentangle the confusing story of his parentage, which had left him with the feeling that he had been fobbed off with lies about his identity, and here at last was an opportunity to discover the truth about himself before he died. He finished his treatment in his own time as soon as he felt able to cope with as much of the truth as he had been able to discover. The panic attacks had not completely gone, nor had he yet come to any definite decision about what to do with risks of further floods and whether he had been wise to move from countryside to town. But he felt able to live with his problems. He made his own evaluation of what therapy had meant to him.

In Chapter 1, I listed some problems, specific to old age and the transitions of later life. The clients described illustrate most of these themes: bereavement, fear of death, having to move house, living alone and loneliness. All these clients were, in varying degrees, depressed, but none of them would have been diagnosed as having a depression in the sense of suffering from an illness. All of them were reacting to loss of some kind (Chapter 9, about loss, is the longest in the book) and the prospect of future diminishment, which any younger person would most probably see as unbearably depressing. What we need to remember is that, over the experiences of a life-time, many old people manage to develop ways of coping that deserve more respect than is usually given to them.

A gap between doctors and counsellors

None of the above clients fits easily into the medical quantitative paradigm, which requires 'measurement, the rigorous use of controls, statistical manipulation of data and replicability' (Wiener and Sher, 1993: 146), all of which may seem irrelevant to those engaged in the actual process of counselling. Fonagy (1993: 577) criticises process research because it depends on acecdotal clinical data. Thus he dismisses the client's story as not worth the researcher's attention. Some counsellors feel driven to believe that their work, by its very nature, does not lend itself to any kind of research methodology. But Wiener and Sher argue that research is a necessity, especially if treatment is to be publicly funded, and that we need to find a new paradigm that complements, instead of being a second-hand substitute for, medical practice.

> Counselling has been deliberately invited into primary care as a diversified resource, seeking not 'cures', but understanding. To merge the evaluation of counselling's effectiveness with medical models is to deny its raison d'être. (Wiener and Sher, 1993: 147)

In many cases, there is no gap. Busy GPs find their practice counsellors are an invaluable resource, a saving both of time and money. Or they may find themselves talking different languages. Where the doctor can only see disease, the counsellor moves in a less tangible world of feeling, story-telling and nameless fear, and the task is to relate holistically to the client, not as a case, but as an individual. If doctors and counsellors manage discussions about their clients/patients, they should be able to respect – and often gain from – each other's difference.

Research and the older client

Not only is there a dearth of research into older people's therapy, but, up till now, hardly enough data to set up a worthwhile project, though some authorities are working in that direction. In the next few years, this situation is likely to change. As the population continues to get older, and ageist attitudes diminish, we may see many more 70 and 80 year-old clients. These will no longer conform to the Victorian stereotypes that we have, for much too long, attached to them, but will be individuals who have kept up with the advances in technology and widened their horizons through greater opportunities to work and to travel than were possible for their predecessors. They will also, most probably, be conversant with psychology, at least to the extent of knowing something about what they are committing themselves to when they come into counselling. This new generation of elders may be no more embarrassed than their juniors if asked whether they mind their sessions being recorded, or invited to fill in a questionnaire. At present, we may find ourselves wanting to protect them from these intrusions, but this shows an (unconscious) ageist bias in ourselves. These clients, we feel, have not grown up with tape recorders and may hold paranoid fantasies about being spied upon, should they be introduced. Are these old people paranoid? Sometimes, in their helplessness, it may seem that they are, or, if they are, is it a reaction to the way we treat them? When more older people begin coming into therapy and are no longer ashamed of doing so, I see no reason for them to resent talking about themselves to researchers, provided there is no compulsion and their privacy is not felt to be invaded. If telling their stories comes naturally, they may be gratified that those who listen seem to find what they have to say worth hearing, and be flattered perhaps at being asked to participate.

But, in answering the question 'How do we evaluate old-age counselling?' I can only say that we will have to wait a few years for the answer.

Reflection and review

- If you were in the position of being a client, would you be willing to participate in a research project by talking to the researcher about how you felt your counselling was progressing? How easy or difficult might you find it to say no?
- Now think of asking one of your older clients to participate. How do you think he or she would react to filling up a questionnaire before and after treatment, or being subjected to an intensive interview with a researcher perceived as a stranger?
- Do you see the outcome of therapy as (a) a cure from symptoms or (b) an increase in self-understanding? What sort of research do you think appropriate in the case of (b)?

12

Some Useful Exercises

These exercises are part of a (largely humanistic) counselling tradition, and their unpublished origins are often impossible to trace. Those described here have been adapted by me as suitable for older clients and their counsellors. There are many variations on the themes of guided fantasy, telling stories, expressing emotions and understanding dreams. My hope is that counsellors working in this field may use what I have written as suggestions for further adaptation to suit particular groups of counsellors, students and clients.

For counsellors and students A group exercise to enable the participants to look into themselves and their own attitudes to old-age and death. Not suitable for use with clients. Sit quietly for 15 to 20 minutes and imagine yourself 20 years older than you are now. Where will you be living? How will you be spending your time – and who with? In your imagination, think about all the changes that will have taken place over 20 years, both in the outside world and in yourself. Think about loss and bereavement. Take a few minutes to mourn your own losses – of people near to you who have died, of your youthful energy which you may feel is ebbing away. Do you tire easily? Are you aware of aches and pains, diminishment of sight and hearing? Do people treat you differently? What does it feel like to become the older generation in your family? Now, try and let the losses go. Concentrate on what you feel you have gained – freedom? Wisdom? Or the more tangible blessings such as grandchildren? Think also about facing death. Are you afraid? What would you like to leave behind for family and friends?

The leader should take you through these stages slowly to help you in your silence, while watching each member of the group for possible signs of distress. There is no need to stick to a set time. I have found it helpful if individuals can catch the leader's eye and nod when they feel ready to move on, either to share their feelings with the group, or, if they prefer, to sit still and listen before joining in a discussion of what has been experienced.

I find this exercise works best in a group of 10 to 15 members, who feel helped by each other's shared experiences. The facilitator needs to be sensitive enough for the group to feel held and supported. If, through illness or shortened life-expectancy, any member feels unable to contemplate being alive in 20 years' time, a shorter term might be suggested, or if, for any other reason, the exercise is likely to be too stressful, it should be made clear that each participant has the freedom to drop out.

In bringing the session to a close, the leader needs to highlight the differences in individual expectations, so that, in our work with clients, we should be aware of differing attitudes to ageing and death, and reminded of the unhelpfulness of such responses as 'I know just how you feel'.

Guided fantasy – journeys These are often helpful both for counsellors and clients, either individually or in groups, and can take many forms. As we grow older we look back on our lives and the metaphor of a journey often comes to mind. Dante, when he wrote his *Divine Comedy*, described how, in mid-life, he found himself in a dark wood. A wood of some kind, dark or light, is quite a good starting point. The exercise that follows shows how this, and other metaphors, can be used, though I suggest that any interpreting should be left to the individual concerned.

Imagine yourself walking through a wood. Notice the trees and any clearings you find between them. Does the light come through? Is it a place where you might lose your way? Go on walking but look down at the path, where you will find two things – a key, and, a bit later, a cup. Notice what they are like and make a picture in your mind of both objects. Are they out of the ordinary? Might they be useful?

Continue on your path and you will be aware of an animal coming up behind you – a bear perhaps, or a wild boar. What do you do? Eventually you come to a river. You have several choices. What do you choose to do? Lastly you come to a house. Again you have choices. You don't know if anyone lives there. Perhaps it is empty. You may or may not be curious. I wonder what you choose to do.

The story-teller has posed quite a lot of questions, but suggests leaving the answers till the end, when the individual making this journey is invited to try and make sense of the experience, and perhaps, through the story, discover some new insights about his or her life. The wood, the key, the cup, the bear, the river and the house can all be powerful metaphors, whose meanings vary with each individual, so it is important not to impose the story-teller's personal view.

Other fantasy journeys may involve climbing mountains, exploring caves, consulting wise men or women, talking to birds or animals, looking for hidden treasure. Traditional fairy tales, because of their archetypal character, may remind us of fears and values remembered from childhood. In a group setting, the leader invites members to recall their favourite stories and what special meanings they had for each member of the group.

Life-lines I owe this exercise to Josefine Speyer's workshops at The Natural Death Centre. This exercise can be an aid to reminiscence in that it enables each participant to assess the best and worst of his or her life-experience and to discern particular themes that may indicate future progress. For the older client, there will inevitably be more emphasis on the past than on long-term goals, and on finding meaning in the life that has been lived. I suggest that counsellors intending to use this exercise with older clients should first try it on themselves and monitor the mixture of feelings that will emerge. Drawing life-lines sometimes features on counselling training courses in order to heighten self-awareness.

Take a big sheet of paper and draw a straight line across the middle. Write your date of birth on the left and today's date on the far right at the line's other end. Now fill in important dates in your life in chronological order, briefly describing what happened, using a red pen for good memories and black for bad (or, if you prefer, writing bad memories below the line and good ones above). You may have to continue on another sheet of paper. Your last entry can be about how you feel at the present time and what you are still looking forward to experiencing – not necessarily in the distant future, but perhaps next week or even tomorrow.

When you have finished, discuss with the counsellor (or the group) how you felt while doing the exercise and what you feel now having completed it.

I would not recommend this exercise without giving the client/student time to talk about it afterwards.

Anger   Many of our older clients are not accustomed to expressing anger. They were brought up to hide their feelings, especially in public, and were supposed to fit into what were considered appropriate roles according to their sex, age and station in life. Children and adolescents were taught to obey their parents and not to argue with people of an older generation. Not surprisingly, anger, frustration and bitterness often seethed beneath a placid surface without ever boiling over into angry words or actions. Women, especially, had good reason for being angry at their treatment as second-class citizens. The rigid class system kept people in fixed positions, often without complaint. In spite of the changes in society that gradually came about during the second half of the 20th century, poverty and lack of education still affect many of today's older population, especially those from ethnic minorities, who face continuing discrimination.

The following exercises come from a colleague, Marie Little, who has run anger workshops in Sussex. She agrees with me that some of the techniques used in her groups could function in a liberating way to put older people in touch with their suppressed feelings. The exercises could be used either in groups or one to one. Students and student counsellors can also be greatly helped in understanding themselves and their clients.

1   What do you associate with the word 'anger'? Think of some of the words that are used about anger – what do they mean for you personally? Write some of them down and share them with a partner or with the group.
2   Allow yourself to be a two year-old, having a 'paddy'. In a safe place, try stamping and screaming. Then take time to think about how that felt and whether tantrums were ever 'allowed' in your family. Think how powerful these could be. How does it feel for you now – OK or a bit scary? (*I advise going cautiously with this one. Releasing years of pent-up rage might get alarmingly out of control. AO*)

3   Who was the angry adult in your family? How was anger expressed and how did it make you feel? Remember occasions when family members expressed their angry feelings and whether this has affected how you express anger as an adult.
4   Make a list of 'Life Statements' consisting of all the hurtful and put-down remarks that people made to you as a child. Then share these with a partner. If you have a long list, take your time – the memory may release a lot of emotion. When you are ready, imagine yourself telling one of these people, who put you down, exactly how the remark made you feel as a child and also how it feels now (exercises by Marie Little in, 1992/3).

Anger is still taboo in many families and, at any age, the exercises can be powerful and release a lot of pain. You need a safe environment with plenty of time for discussion and sharing of experience.

Dream work   I remember supervising a student counsellor who told me that her client had brought a dream to the session. 'But I told her that counsellors aren't trained to interpret dreams.' I remember retorting, 'Who said anything about interpreting?' And I wondered how she would have felt if her own dreams had been similarly dismissed. My suggestion was that she should treat the dream in the same way as any other client material. In this case, her client had taken the trouble to remember her dream and write it down, so it must have, in some way, been important to her. Perhaps this student was overawed by the size of Freud's famous tome, *The Interpretation of Dreams*, or by Jung's extensive knowledge of mythology. I put it to her that the least she could do was listen, take an interest and find out what ideas the client herself might have about the dream, as well as possible associations with her waking life. Human beings, I commented, have always been fascinated by these mysterious 'visions of the night', as one only has to read the Bible to find out. We could never expect to solve the whole mystery but we might pick up some hints as to possible meanings.

There are many ways of exploring dreams. Neither gestalt nor Jungian therapists agree with Freud that the manifest content (the story told by the dreamer) should be dismissed in favour of the latent content, whose unconscious meaning could only be revealed through analysis. Nor does anyone (even the Freudian) any longer see all dreams as wish fulfilments. Jung introduced the idea of the compensatory nature of dreams, and how they may show an opposite way of being to that of the dreamer's waking consciousness. It is also worth treating the different characters in the dream as aspects of the dreamer's self.

The explorations described here are suitable for individual counselling as well as groups. The following shows a dream group in action.

The leader asks a volunteer to recount a dream. He/she is then asked to repeat the account using the present tense. This gives the group a chance of absorbing what has been said and bringing a sense of immediacy to the story. It is then suggested that the dreamer should identify with one of the dream images, either with a person who appears to be other than herself, or with an animal or some inanimate object. She is then asked to tell the dream again from the point of view of the person or thing she has chosen.

After this, there should be a group discussion to see what further light has been shed on the dream's mystery, and also to support the dreamer if the experience has been intense.

In one case, the dreamer chose some coloured glass which, at the beginning of her dream, she saw in a shop and was not allowed to buy. She told the story from the viewpoint of the glass, who was left out (by not being bought) of the rest of the dream. Being 'left out', brittle, coloured and transparent, certainly produced insight, while leaving the rest of the dream unexplored. Group discussion focused on the 'left out' theme, which was seen to recur in the climax of a complicated story, in which the 'I' telling the dream could not follow her dead husband (alive in the dream) to what was described as 'The Sanctuary'. This dreamer was in her 70s and often dreamed of dead friends.

Enactments   Images from dreams can take physical forms that we can paint, depict in sand trays, or write poems about. Jung made model canals in the mud on the lake shore. As adults, we may be self-conscious and put up resistance to what we think of as 'childish pursuits'. We seem too often to have lost the 'as if' ability, which comes naturally to children. But their play is something we have all experienced early in our lives and we need to find again the spontaneity that has been spoilt by self-criticism and too much concern with artistic merit.

There may be a strong desire to communicate with figures, both real and imaginery, whom we meet in our dreams. Writing letters to the dead, who so often appear in old people's dreams, may be a liberating way of expressing affection or resolving guilt by saying now what we failed to say to them in life. Sometimes there may be recurrent dreams in which, it seems, a conflict needs to be resolved. To quote an example – an ageing dreamer found herself involved in nightly searches for a friend who had died 50 years before. In the dreams, this friend was absent but not dead, and there seemed no reason why they never met. Eventually, the message from the dream seemed to get through and the dreamer went searching (in her waking life) for her friend's grave. When she found it, she felt that she had laid her friend to rest and the dreams stopped.

Psychodreama is a way of enacting dreams in group therapy, with members taking different roles in a selected dream, and the dreamer either taking part or (with the therapist) helping to stage manage the event. The enactment may seem to move far away from the dream, as dreamt, and yet serve to amplify its complex imagery through the interactions of the players.

Active imagination   is a Jungian technique for using imagination in a controlled way. This is something that we have all done as children, through elaborating our fantasies so that they seem real, and, in fact, treating them as really happening, but without losing the essential 'as if ' ability that makes us remain conscious of what we are doing.

> If one is attacked by a dragon in active imagination, it is against the rules to say 'only imagination' and turn the dragon into a poodle ... Active imagination correctly done, goes beyond the sense of 'I'm doing it' and shows that the imaginal objects and persons begin to act with surprising autonomy. (Hall, 1991: 341–2)

Active imagination can be used on waking to continue the dream's story by amplifying its contents. There is a discipline in not letting the mind drift away from the images, and the dreamer needs to have a strong enough ego to stay with the scene as it unfolds. Whatever the age of the client, counsellors must be able to determine whether this exercise would be helpful or not. Old people, like children, can frighten themselves with their own imaginings, and in some cases, this is not worth risking.

Relaxation   What follows is a simple technique that has been used successfully with people suffering pain of all kinds as well as discomfort and stress. It is worth practising to get the habit of deep relaxation, when needed.

1   Get comfortable in a chair which supports your back, arms and head and doesn't let your feet dangle. Be sure you are not too warm or too cold, not sitting in a draught and not bothered by the light shining in your eyes. Try to pick a time when you won't be interrupted.
2   Do a body check. Is any bit of you uncomfortable? Shake, wriggle and relax.
3   Close your eyes, or focus on a distant object level with your gaze.
4   Imagine you are a puppet and someone has tied your strings in a tight knot at the back of your head. How does it feel?
5   Now imagine that the knot is unravelling. Slowly, the tightness goes, beginning in your head, face and neck and travelling across your shoulders and down your arms, into your hands. As the strings loosen, your forehead feels cool and light, but your face, neck, shoulders, arms and hands feel loose, warm and heavy. Repeat to yourself: loose, warm, heavy, as the feeling spreads. Now let the looseness spread down your chest, back and tummy into your hips, bottom and legs. Keep repeating loose, warm, heavy to yourself as you unwind and relax more and more deeply. Let the feeling spread right down to your feet and toes: loose, warm, heavy.
6   When you are warm and floppy all over, think about your breathing. Imagine you are standing at the top of a flight of broad, shallow steps down into a garden. You are going to breathe down the steps. On step 1, breathe in gently and evenly, and float across the step. Breathe out to sink gently down to step 2. Carry on down the steps, breathing in to float and out to sink, until you reach the garden at the bottom.
7   When you are ready to come out of your relaxation, breathe back up the steps, this time breathing in to float up each step, and out to drift across it.
8   When you reach the top of the steps, open your eyes, stretch and give a little shake before you get up. While you have been relaxing, your blood pressure will have dropped and your heart rate will have slowed down, so don't jump up all at once – take it easy!

9   Practice makes perfect. Try to set a time aside every day to relax for 10 to 15 minutes at least, and you will soon be able to become deeply relaxed very easily. Use music if it helps.

10   Enjoy it!

(Lewith and Horne, 1987)

The above was introduced to SAGE counsellors on a study day taken by Sandra Horne.

Some Suggestions for Further Reading

On Old Age

For an exhaustive study of how it feels to be old and how society has treated its senior citizens, I recommend Simone de Beauvoir's *Old Age*, (1970, London: Penguin).

Betty Friedan's *The Fountain of Age* (1993, London: Jonathan Cape) gives a more up-to-date American view.

M. Featherstone and A. Wernick *Images of Ageing: Cultural Representations in Later Life* (1985, London and New York: Routledge).

On Death

John Hinton's standard work *Dying* (first published in 1967, and republished in 1990; London: Penguin) gives a medical view, as does Sherwin Nuland's *How We Die* (1994, London: Chatto & Windus), with its clearly defined descriptions of death.

Elizabeth Kübler Ross *On Death and Dying* (1970, London: Tavistock) has become a standard textbook in the helping professions.

Ernest Becker *The Denial of Death* (1973, New York: The New Press) gives a post-Freudian study of the psychology of death.

Ann Orbach *Life, Psychotherapy and Death* (1999, London: Jessica Kingsley).

Counselling Older People

I include D.P. McAdam's *The Stories We Live By: Personal Myths and the Making of the Self* (1993, London and New York: Guilford Press) as a useful introduction to narrative therapy, even though not written particularly with older people in mind.

Ann Orbach *Not too Late: Psychotherapy and Ageing* (1996, London: Jessica Kingsley) gives a psychodynamic study of therapy with older people.

Steve Scrutton *Counselling Older People: A Creative Response to Ageing* (1994, London: Edward Arnold), and also his *Bereavement and Grief: Supporting Older People through Loss* (1995, London: Edward Arnold).

Paul Terry *Counselling the Elderly and their Carers* (1997, London: Macmillan) is an interesting account of working as psychologist and counsellor in a geriatric hospital.

Working with Ethnic Minority Elders

Y. Alibhai-Brown *Caring for Ethnic Minority Elders: A Guide* (1998, Age Concern: England) is an excellent introduction to the subject.

References

Albery, N., Elliot, G. and Elliot, J. (1977) *The Natural Death Handbook*. London, Sydney, Auckland, Johannesburg: Rider.

Alibhai-Brown, Y. (1998) *Caring for Ethnic Minority Elders: A Guide*. London: Age Concern.

Ashley, P.M. and Barrett, P.W. (1997) *A Life Worth Living: Practical Strategies for Reducing Depression in Older Adults*. London, Toronto, Sydney: Health Education Press.

Beck, A.T. (1976) *Cognitive Therapy and Emotional Disorders*. Harmondsworth: Penguin.

Becker, E. (1973) *The Denial of Death*. New York: Macmillan.

Bennet, A. and Cass, B. (1998) *Counselling Work with Older People: A Report on Behalf of Age Concern England's Activ/Age Unit*. London: Age Concern.

Bowlby, J. (1969) *Attachment and Loss, Vol. 1: Attachment*. New York: Basic Books.

Bowlby, J. (1980) *Attachment and Loss: Loss, Sadness and Depression*. London: Hogarth Press.

Brotherton, C. (1995) *Social and Legal Context of Counselling*. Diploma in Independent Professional Counselling. West Sussex: Institute of Higher Education.

Buber, M. (1970) *I and Thou*. Edinburgh: T & T Clark.

Burton, M. (1998) *Psychotherapy and Primary Health Care: Assessment for Brief or Longer Term Treatment*. Chichester: Wiley.

Butler, R.N. (1963) 'The Life Review: An Interpretation of Reminiscence in Ageing', *Psychiatry*, 26: 67–75.

Butler, R.N. (1975) 'The Elderly: An Overview', *American Journal of Psychiatry*: 132.

Butler, R.N. and Lewis, M.I. (1974) 'Life Review Therapy', *Geriatrics*: 65–75.

Butler, M. and Orbach, A. (1993) *Being Your Age: Pastoral Care for Older People*. London: SPCK.

Casement, P. (1985) *On Learning from the Patient*. London, New York, Tavistock.

Chester, R. and Smith, J. (1997) *Older People's Sadness*. London: Counsel and Care.

Comfort, A. (1977) *A Good Age*. London: Michael Beazley.

Counsel and Care (1994) *Being Cared For: A Discussion Document About Old People With Depression Living at Home*. London: Counsel and Care.

Cummings, E. and Henry, W.E. (1961) *The Process of Disengagement*. New York: Basic Books.

Davanloo, H. (1980) *Short-Term Psychodynamic Psychotherapy*. New York: Jason Aronson.

Ellis, A. (1962) *Cognitive Therapy and Emotional Disorders*. Harmondsworth: Penguin.

Erikson, E. (1959) 'Identity and the Life-Cycle', *Psychological Issues*, Monograph 1.

Erikson, E. (1974) *Childhood and Society*. Harmondsworth: Penguin.

Etherington, K. (2000) *Narrative Approaches to Working with Adult Survivors of Child Sexual Abuse: the Client's, the Counsellor's and the Researcher's Story*. London: Jessica Kingsley.

Etherington, K. (2001) 'Writing Qualitative Research: a Gathering of Selves', *Counselling Psychotherapy Research*, 1 (2): 119–25.

Featherstone, M. and Wernick, A. (1985) *Images of Ageing: Cultural Representations of Later Life*. London and New York: Routledge.

Fonagy, P. (1993) 'Psychoanalytic and Empirical Approach to Developmental Psychology: Can They be Usefully Integrated?' *Journal of the Royal Society of Medicine*, 86: 577–81.

Fonagy, P. (1996) 'Psychoanalysis and Attachment Theory', in J. Cassidy and P. Shaver (eds), *Handbook of Attachment*. London: Guildford.

Frankl, V. (1987) *Man's Search for Meaning*. London: Hodder & Stroughton.

Freud, S. (1895) 'Psychotherapy of Hysteria', in S. Freud and J. Breuer (1974) *Studies in Hysteria*. Harmondsworth: Penguin.

Freud, S. and Breuer, J. (1974) *Studies in Hysteria*. Harmondsworth: Penguin.

Friedan, B. (1993) *The Fountain of Age*. London: Jonathan Cape.

Fyro, K., Hardell, C., Westlund Cederroth, K. (1999) 'Problem-Oriented Sessions: Presentation of a Method for Therapeutic Work in a Narrow Frame', *Psychodynamic Counselling*, 5 (4): 465–81.

GAD (1998) *Based National Populations Projection*. London: Government Actuary's Department.

Gilchrist, C. (1999) *Turning Your Back on Us: Older People in the NHS*. London: Age Concern.

Gilleard, C.J. (1984) *Living with Dementia: Community Care of the Elderly Mentally Infirm*. Beckenham, Kent and Surrey Hills; NSW, Australia: Croom Helm.

Goncalves, O.F. (1995) 'Cognitive Narrative Psychotherapy: the Hermeneutic Construction of Alternative Meanings', in M.J. Mahoney (ed.), *Cognitive and Constructive Psychotherapies: Theory, Research and Practice*. New York: Springer. pp. 139–62.

Greenson, R. (1974) *The Technique and Practice of Psychoanalysis*. London: Hogarth.

Gross, S. (1999) 'The Place of Therapy in Training', *Psychodynamic Counselling*, 5 (1): 123.

Haight, B.K. and Burnside, I. (1993) 'Reminiscence and Life Review: Explaining the Difference', *Archives of Psychiatric Nursing*, 7: 91–8.

Hall, J. (1991) *Patterns of Dreaming: Jungian Techniques in Theory and Practice*. Boston and London: Shambola

Hartley, L.P. (1953) *The Go Between*. London: Hamish Hamilton.

Haviland, W. (1975) *Cultural Anthropology*. New York: Holt, Rinehart & Winston.

Hawkins, P. and Shohet, R. (1989) *Supervision in the Helping Professions: An Individual and Organisational Approach*. Milton Keynes: Open University Press.

Henry, W.P., Schact, T.E., Strupp, H.H., Butler, S.F. and Binder, J.R. (1993) 'Effects of Training in Time-Limited Dynamic Psychotherapy: Changes in Therapist Behaviour', *Journal of Constructive Clinical Psychology*, 61: 434–40.

Hinton, J. (1990) *Dying*. Harmondsworth: Penguin. (First published 1967).

Holmes, J. (2000) 'Attachment Theory and Psychoanalysis: A Rapprochement', *British Jounal of Psychotherapy*, 7 (2): 157–72.

Hyer, L.A. and Sohnle, S.J. (2001) *Trauma Among Older People: Issues and Treatment*. Philadelphia, Hove: Brunner-Routledge.

Jacobs, M. (1982) *Still Small Voice: An Introduction to Pastoral Counselling*. London: SPCK.

Jerome, D. (1994) 'Family Estrangement: Parents and Children who "Lose Touch"', *Journal of Family Therapy*, 16 (3).

Jung, C.G. (1967) *Memories, Dreams, Reflections*. London: Fontana.

Jung, C.G. (1990) *Symbols of Transformation, CW5*. London: Routledge.

Jung, C.G. (1977) *The Structure and Dynamics of the Psyche, CW8*. London: Routledge.

Kelly, G.A. (1955) *The Psychology of Personal Constructs*, Vol. 1 & 2. New York: Norton.

Killick, J. (1994) *Please Give Me Back My Personality: Writing and Dementia*. Stirling: University of Stirling.

Kohut, H. and Wolf, E. (1978) 'The Disorders of the Self and their Treatment: An Outline', *International Journal of Psychoanalysis*, 54: 413–25.

Kübler-Ross, E. (1970) *On Death and Dying*. London: Tavistock.

Lashley, M.E. (1993) 'The Painful Side of Reminiscence', *Geriatric Nursing*, 14 (3): 138–41.

Lee, W.M.L. (1999) *An Introduction to Multicultural Counselling*. Philadelphia, London: Accelerated Development (Taylor & Francis Group).

Lewith, G.T. and Horne, S. (1987) *Drug-free Pain Relief*. Wellingborough: Thorsons.

Lomax, E. (1996) *The Railway Man*. London: Vintage.

Luborsky, L. and Crits-Christoph, P. (eds) (1990) *Understanding Transference: The CCRT Method*. New York: Basic Books.

McAdams, D.P. (1993) *The Stories We Live By: Personal Myths and the Making of the Self*. London, New York: Guilford Press.

McLeod, J. (1998) *An Introduction to Counselling*, second edition. Buckingham, Philadelphia. Open University Press:

Mahrer, A.R., Nadler, W.P., Dessaulles, A., Gervaize, P.A., Sterner, J. (1987) 'Good and Very Good Moments in Psychotherapy: Content, Distribution and Facilitation', *Psychotherapy*, 24: 7–14.

Main, M. and Goldwyn, S. (1995) 'Interview-Based Adult Attachment', *Developmental Psychology*, 19: 227–39.

Malan, D.H. (1976) *The Frontiers of Brief Therapy*. New York: Plenum Press.

Malan, D.H. (1979) *Individual Psychotherapy and the Science of Psychodynamics*. London: Butterworth.

Maluccio, A. (1979) *Learning from Clients: Interpersonal Helping as Viewed by Clients and Social Workers*. New York: Free Press.

Mander, G. (2000) 'Beginnings, Endings and Outcomes: A Comparison of Methods and Goals', *Psychodynamic Counselling*, 6 (3): 301–17.

Martin, P. (2000) 'It Takes Two to Tango: Research and Practice in an Amazing Dance', *Counselling and Psychotherapy Research*, 1 (3): 163–5.

Mellor-Clark, J. (1997) 'Evaluating Effectiveness: Needs, Problems and Potential Benefits', paper presented at the BAC Counselling Research Conference, Birmingham, 14 June, 1997.

Orbach, A. (1996) *Not Too Late: Psychotherapy and Ageing*. London: Jessica Kingsley.

Parlett, M. and Hemming, J. (1996) 'Gestalt Therapy', in W. Dryden (ed.), *A Handbook of Individual Therapy*. London: Sage.

Plato (translated by J. Llewellin Davies) (1908) *The Republic of Plato*. London: Macmillan.

Polkinhorne, D.E. (1992) 'Post Modern Epistemology of Practice', in S. Kate (ed.), *Psychology and Postmodernism*. London: Sage.

Rennie, D.L. (1990) 'Towards a Representation of the Client's Experience of the Psychotherapeutic Hour', in G. Lietaer, J. and R. Rombauts Van Balen (eds), *Client-Centred and Experiential Therapy in the Nineties*. Leuven, Belgium: Leuven University Press. pp. 155–72.

Rennie, D.L. (1992) 'Qualitative Analysis of Client's Experience of Psychotherapy: the Unfolding of Reflexivity', in S.G. Toukmanian and D.L. Rennie (eds), *Psychotherapy Process Research: Paradigmatic and Narrative Approaches*. Thousand Oaks CA: Sage.

Rogers, C.R. (1963) 'The Concept of the Fully Functioning Person', *Psychotherapy: Theory, Research and Practice*, 1: 17–26.

Rogers, C.R. (1978) *On Personal Power: Inner Strength and its Revolutionary Impact.* London: Constable.

Roth, A. and Fonagy, P. with Parry, G., Target, M. and Woods, R. (1996) *What Works for Whom: A Critical View of Psychotherapy Research.* New York: Guilford Press.

Scott-Maxwell, F. (1968) *The Measure of My Days.* London: Stuart & Wilkins.

Scrutton, S. (1995) *Bereavement and Grief: Supporting Older People Through Loss.* London, Sydney, Auckland: Edward Arnold (Hodder Headline Group).

Scrutton, S. (1998) *Counselling Older People: A Creative Response to Ageing.* London: Edward Arnold.

Stirling, E. (1996) 'Social Role Valorisation: Making a Difference to the Lives of Older People', in R.T. Woods (ed.), *Handbook of Clinical Psychology and Ageing.* Chichester: Wiley.

Storr, A. (1989) *Solitude.* London: Flamingo.

Strauss, A. and Corbin, J. (1990) *Basics of Qualitative Research: Grounded Theory Procedures and Techniques.* London: Sage.

Terry, P. (1997) *Counselling the Elderly and their Carers.* London: Macmillan.

Thompson, D. (1993) *Mental Illness: The Fundamental Facts.* London: Mental Health Foundation.

Tomer, H. (2000) 'Closing Thoughts and Open Questions', in H. Tomer (ed.), *Death Attitudes and Older Adults.* Pensylvania: Brunner Routledge.

Vaughan, P. (2002) 'Age Cannot Wither Them', *The Guardian*, 13/3/02.

Walter, T. (1994) *The Revival of Death.* London, New York: Routledge.

West, W. (2001) 'Beyond Grounded Theory: The Use of a Heuristic Approach to Qualitative Research', *Counselling and Psychotherapy Research*, 1 (2): 29–39.

Wiener, J. and Sher, M. (1993) *Counselling and Psychotherapy in Primary Health Care: A Psychodnamic Approach.* London: Macmillan.

Winnicott, D.W. (1941) 'The Observation of Infants in a Set Situation', in D.W. Winnicott, *Collected Papers: Through Paediatrics to Psychoanalyis.* London: Hogarth.

Winnicott, D.W. (1958) 'The Capacity to be Alone', in D.W. Winnicott, *The Maturational Processes and the Facilitating Environment: Studies in the Theory of Emotional Development.* London: Hogarth.

Winnicott, D.W. (1971) *Playing and Reality.* Harmondsworth: Penguin.

Worsthorne, P. (2000) *The Guardian*, 4/4/2000.

Zera, D. (1992) 'Coming of Age in a Heterosexual World: The Development of Gay and Lesbian Adolescents', *Adolescence*, 27: 849–54.

Index